BEYOND
FLIGHT
or FIGHT

A Compassionate Guide
for Working with Fearful Dogs

BEYOND
FLIGHT
or FIGHT

Sunny Weber

Beyond Flight or Fight:
A Compassionate Guide for Working with Fearful Dogs
Published by Pups and Purrs Press
Denver, CO

Library of Congress Control Number: 2015948183
Weber, Sunny, Author
Beyond Flight or Fight: A Compassionate Guide for Working with Fearful Dogs

ISBN: 978-0-9966612-1-8
Dogs / Training

QUANTITY PURCHASES: Animal rescues, schools, companies, professional groups, clubs, and other organizations may qualify for special terms when ordering quantities of this title. For information, email the author directly at Sunny@SunnyWeber.com.

PUPS & PURRS
PRESS

DENVER, CO

Dedication

To my muse and soul-mate,
a timid Australian Shepherd
named Miles who shared his life
with me for fifteen-and-a-half years.

Table of Contents

Acknowledgments   i

Introduction   v

Chapter 1: What is Fear?   **1**
   Fear as a Primary Emotion   3
   Fear as a Secondary Emotion   6

Chapter 2: Rescued! Now What?   **11**
   The Structures of Rescue Organizations   11
   The Case for Relationship Building   14
   Nature vs. Nurture in Fear Development   15
   Shelter Behavior Modification Programs   16
   The Advantage of Foster Homes   21

**Chapter 3: Beginning Rehabilitation
          with a Fearful Dog**   **25**
   How to Begin Rehabilitation   30
   Departures from Routine   32
   Safe Places   33
   Desensitization   35
   The Basic Key to Behavior Modification   36
   How a Dog Senses Fear Stimuli   36
   Discovering Fear Triggers   40

Chapter 4: Over Threshold   **45**
   Over Threshold   47
   Purposeful Flooding   47
   Catatonic Behavior   49
   Fear Aggression   49

Accidental Flooding   52
Human Flooding Response vs.
   Dog Flooding Response   53

Chapter 5: The Importance of a Familiar Handler   57
Learning to Trust One Person   60

Chapter 6: The Importance of Time   65
What Time Can Do   69

Chapter 7: The Importance of Leadership   75
The Role of Leadership   79
Canine Behavior and Leadership   81
Fear Dominance vs. Leadership   82
Do Dogs Rebel Against Leadership?   84
Punishment   85
Correction   86
Reconnection with the Leader   87

Chapter 8: Learning Theory   91
The ABCs of Learning Theory and
   Rehabilitation   92
Habituation and Curiosity   95
Desensitizing Fearful Dogs   96

Chapter 9: Self-Confidence and Advocacy   99
Self-Confidence   100
Supporting the Timid Dog   101
Protecting Your Pet   103
Appropriate Advocacy   104

Chapter 10: Habituating a Fearful Dog to People   109
Approach   110

Initial and Early Stages of Contact   113
Collaring and Leashing   115
Grooming   116
Movement and Calming   119
Mirror and Displacement Activity   120
Voice as a Tool   124
Dovetailing Voice, Emotion, and Training   132

Chapter 11: Training the Fearful Dog   135
Emotional and Ego Control in Training   136
Correction and Redirection   137
The Most Important Command   140
Training Tools   143
Correction Cues   145
Using Dog Social Psychology to Correct   150
Understanding Nonresponse   151
Repetition for Fluency   154
Proofing for Reliability   155
Startle/Recovery Ratios   156
Backing Up   157
Trainer Emotional Fitness   159

Chapter 12: Realistic Evaluation   161
The First Week   162
The Second Week   163
Weeks Three and Four   164
Getting to Know You   165
What to Settle For   166
Moving On   168
Determine What the Optimal Level Is   170
Giving Up   173

Conclusion   179

Glossary of Terms   183

—)|(—

Acknowledgments

My appreciation goes to those who have influenced, encouraged, and guided me in my mission to save fearful dogs' lives. To Dick Gasaway, my dog training mentor, who taught me not to *train* dogs, but to *read* dogs. His positive approaches were ahead of their time and saved many dogs from cruel treatment and many handlers from ignorant heartache.

To the Dumb Friends League Shelter in Denver, Colorado, who generously provided me with the opportunities to work with many dogs, cats, and horses who needed second, third and fourth chances.

To the Best Friends Animal Sanctuary in Kanab, Utah, Kindness Ranch in Hartville, Wyoming, Blue Rose Ranch Horse Rescue in Springfield, Colorado, National Mill Dog Rescue in Peyton, Colorado, and all the other rescues, sanctuaries, shelters, and publications who graciously allowed me to volunteer, advise, write for, and work with their animals.

Thanks beyond words go to my writing coaches and teachers at Lighthouse Writers in Denver, Colorado.

More thanks go to my publishing team, without whom I would still be circling my wagons, unable to decipher direction. To Melanie Mulhall, my editor at Dragonheart Writing and Editing for helping my words shine; Helena Mariposa, my proof-reader at Mariposa Book Transformation Services; Polly Letofsky, my publishing coach at My Word Publishing; Mary Walewski, my social media coach at Buy The Book Marketing; Corrinda Campbell, my webmistress at Small Business WP Services; Nick Zelinger, my cover designer at NZ Graphics; and Andrea Costantine, my interior designer at Self-Publishing Experts.

Abundant appreciation goes to all the authors, trainers, and behaviorists who came before me and fired my passion with their actions, words, activism, and influence, including but not limited to: Patricia McConnell, Temple Grandin, Suzanne Hetts, Dan Estep, Pamela Reid, Turid Rugaas, Desmond Morris, Suzanne Clothier, Jean Donaldson, Nicole Wilde, Ian Dunbar, Roger Abrantes, Bruce Fogle, Nicolas Dodman, Carole Lea Benjamin, and Barbara Woodhouse.

My sincerest gratitude goes to all the dogs who taught me by allowing me into their lives and hearts, and who honored me with their trust. Without these humble, sometimes woebegone, and always homeless dogs, I would not have found my mission in life, nor been able to find my own education in their eyes, body language and silent, yet articulate communication.

—ↄ丨ↄ—

Introduction

Sampson the Yorkshire terrier huddled in the corner of his enclosure in my family room. Freed after nine years in a puppy mill with no human contact except when grabbed and carried to the breeding cage, he stared at me with cataract-clouded bug eyes. His tongue lolled out the left side of his mouth because the shelter veterinarians had pulled all his rotten teeth out. He froze, then cowered with his scrawny tail tucked. Could I gain this pitiful creature's trust? Would I be able to help him become "adoptable?" Could I save his life?

When I began my professional career in dog training, my goal was to save dogs from euthanasia and help them find quality lives. For ten years I attended classes, conferences, and clinics. I hired mentors to work one-on-one with me and my own three dogs, who were my guinea pigs and graciously forgave my mistakes as I learned dog training and behavior. I competed in obedience, performed at pet fairs, became involved with pet visitation, and networked with loosely knit small groups of people on similar missions. I owned my own business in a field I had reached the pinnacle of, and as my enthusiasm for that work cooled, a long dormant fire within me rekindled. Ever since childhood, I had felt a deep kinship with animals.

My goals gradually evolved. I worked towards financial stability, so I could afford to transition my life. I bought a house with a yard, then proceeded to redesign it inside and out for animal care. Eventually, I secured a volunteer position with a nonprofit organization that trained shelter dogs for service with wheelchair-bound clients. Later, a friend and I began a breed rescue. With that organization, I served as the foster caregiver, medical technician, trainer, and adoption counselor. We found homes for every dog we obtained from shelters that had given up on them or run out of room. Along the way I saw the fates of hundreds of homeless rejected dogs. There were not enough rescue groups to save them.

Drawn to the world of high-volume shelter fostering, I cared for dogs, puppies, cats, and kittens. Fostering bought these pets time, especially during the busy seasons (spring, summer, and fall) of mass pet reproduction. The shelter I volunteered for had been a source of service dogs and dogs for our rescue. I had known of their work since my family adopted my first dog there when I was in elementary school. Over the years this shelter had struggled, grown, and made its mark in our region through its innovative programs. It had grown into a model facility, because of its physical design, educational efforts, and business model.

I tested myself at the shelter by becoming a humane educator, providing a foster home, and participating in outreach efforts, media, special events, and fundraising. They taught me how to administer medical care to the severely ill. They provided me the volume of animals and programs I needed to advance my experience, and the more I learned, the more consumed I became by this growing industry. My shelter education helped me formulate solid goals for a professional future quite different from the career that was paying the bills as I pursued my passion for animals.

During those years, "behavior" became the new buzzword. Marine mammal trainers like Karen Pryor revolutionized the old "pop & jerk" dog training methods because as Association of Pet Dog Trainers (APDT) founder Ian Dunbar once said, "You can't push a killer whale around." I was on the ground floor when positive reinforcement training evolved in dog obedience schools. I saw how we could help dogs understand what we asked of them, and how they would willingly comply, when we understood how to motivate them without bullying tactics.

Nowhere were these techniques better suited than with the fearful dogs I fostered. For all the myriad reasons dogs became timid, saving their lives depended on helping them fit into a human world. Removing fear and helping these sad creatures find peace in the company of a human adopter became my goal. I had found my true calling.

My goal with this book is to share what I have learned about working with fearful dogs during the last twenty-five years. I want to contribute the techniques I have been taught, learned through trial and error, and those I have developed on my own. I hope to provide concise shortcuts to knowledge that were not known when I started.

This book is not a step-by-step training manual. This book is about *relationships*—building trust between a fearful dog and trainer. When there is trust between a dog and their person dog lives will be saved and have quality. Although trust erodes fear, trust can be an elusive goal, especially for those animals who have never experienced kindness.

Fear in dogs is the most common problem behavior that causes people to reject them. Throughout this book we will look at the nature of fear in dogs and learn how we can understand this powerful impediment to our relationships with them. We will examine detailed ways to establish trust through kindness and communication through awareness. We will dissect all the ways people can seem overwhelming and threatening to dogs who, for various reasons, feel alienated from the human world they are forced to inhabit. In the end, we will have knowledge and tools to help dogs "fit" and to become the companions people have treasured for thousands of years.

Although the focus of this book is fearful dogs, the methods covered will also work with cats and horses—animals I have also worked with through rescue organizations. I hope that with your assistance, we can help more animals to live longer, more emotionally comfortable lives filled with respect, compassion, companionship, partnership, love, and most of all, a peaceful existence, free of anxiety and insecurity.

Note: Throughout this book I have alternated between male and female dog nouns, rather than using the impersonal and objectified "it." I have also frequently used "who" instead of "that" to lend personhood to dogs. I hope they will forgive me.

―ง|ง―

*Fear's power lies in its ability to make us believe
we are alone, abandoned to the mercy of monsters,
beasts, and demons. To the extent that we discover
strategies to overcome that sense of isolation,
we find courage.*

—Allan J. Hamilton, M.D.
Brain Surgeon, Professor, Horse Trainer & Behaviorist
Rancho Bosque, Tucson, Arizona

~/|\~

CHAPTER 1

What is Fear?

Charles Darwin—explorer, wildlife illustrator, creator of the theory of evolution, and one of the first to study animal behavior—cited six primary emotions in "higher brained" creatures. He defined higher brained creatures as "animals that have an incipient capacity for empathy, logic, language and magnanimity." The six primary emotions he defined were: happiness, surprise, sadness, anger, disgust, and fear.

Dogs fulfill all of Darwin's descriptions of higher brained creatures, and they will be our focus in this book. Sensitive, intelligent, and intensely aware of their surroundings, dogs experience all of Darwin's primary emotions.

There is no mistaking the appearance of a *happy* dog inviting us to play or come close: relaxed, wiggly body; tail wagging madly; tongue lolling; often emitting a variety of vocalizations. *Surprised* dogs may startle, then respond with barking, whining, and attempts to either engage for comfort or run away in apprehension. Often a surprised dog will return to investigate the stimulus that caused its surprise.

It is easy to spot a *sad* dog too: raised eyebrows, drooping ears, slumped postures, and mournful eyes. *Anger* usually manifests in various forms of aggression, which can result from threatened loss of a valued resource or the instinct to protect home, family, or self. Physical anger can manifest in piloerection, a stiff stance, lifted lips, wrinkled nose, squinting eyes, bared teeth, and deep vocalizations. These are canine facial and body movements that humans instinctively find threatening.

Disgust in dogs is more difficult to interpret. Psychologist Abraham Maslow stated in an article in 1932 that dogs he tested rejected raw dog flesh when it was placed before them as a meal. They turned their faces away from the bowls, averted eye contact, and slowly slunk away. No kidding!

Fear in dogs is a major reason that dogs are surrendered to shelters, rescues, and sanctuaries. Fears believed to be unworkable result in more rejection of dogs as pets than aggression, although certain types of aggression are caused by fear. If we can learn more about all the aspects of what makes dogs afraid, we can help them face stimuli that frighten them and create adoptable dogs from rejected misfits.

We will examine every aspect of fear that I have come across in twenty-five years of rehabilitating fearful dogs. My goal is to help you—a confused and well-meaning owner or professional dog handler—address the behavior in dogs that causes them turmoil. Our mutual goal is to help them find comfort and homes.

What did Darwin have to say about fear? What are primitive fear reactions in dogs? What are reasoned dog responses to fear? How do these reactions apply to our relationships with our dogs? How does fear start? What happens as fear takes over the dog's brain and body? How does fear determine the way a dog acts? Let us start at the beginning: how fear works.

FEAR AS A PRIMARY EMOTION

Emotions are based in the primitive limbic areas of a dog's brain, deep in the amygdala section. Primary emotions such as fear are automatic and require no rational thinking to cause physiological and psychological reactions. Fear results from exposure to any stimulus (object or situation) that is perceived by the brain as a threat to survival. The immediate rush of the stress hormones (adrenaline and cortisol) sets off the rapid and instant reflexive responses Darwin coined, "fight or flight." In a dog, these hormones trigger instantaneous readiness to save himself from a harmful scenario and quickly seek and find physical—and therefore emotional—safety. There are two ways a dog can save himself from danger: to engage in aggression to protect himself (fight) or to run away (flight). Most dogs prefer to run than to fight, so I have changed the order of Darwin's theory to "flight or fight."

For example, when a dog is startled by an unrecognized sound, such as clanging pots, a dropped book, or a backfiring car, he may break into a panicked run to escape. His instinct of flight engages before the dog has a chance to reason and understand that a pot, book, or backfire pose no imminent real threat to his survival.

Another example would be when a dog is held tight for an inoculation at the veterinarian's office. Restraint by a person the dog does not know could result in the struggle for freedom that, if not granted, could escalate into an aggressive fight to escape.

Dogs are predator animals. They evolved primarily for fight, not flight, as prey animals, such as horses, did. Human intervention in breeding, especially in dogs, now limits the use of flight. Some breeds are bred for short legs or small stature, which would severely compromise their survival in Darwin's "survival of the fittest" natural world. In Darwin's nineteenth century concept, his principle of natural selection postulated that those who are eliminated in the struggle for existence are the unfit. Complex human interference through selected breeding sped up the development of physical characteristics that have created dogs "unfit" for survival in the natural world, therefore necessitating our care and protection.

Other physical characteristics have combined to limit the safety of dogs in the wild world. A dog's eyes are in the front of his head, which limits vision and renders him vulnerable to attack from over or behind his head and back. The dog's peripheral vision can also be limited, depending on breed structure and grooming trends. However, dogs are capable of an intense gaze wherever their faces point which, when combined with their other superior senses of smell and hearing, form a compilation of sensory input to their brains. That input can trigger a response according to the brain's determination of what action is needed. That response may include further docile visual, auditory, and olfactory monitoring of a questionable stimulus. If intense fear is triggered, the response could result in the dog's behavior escalating into fight instinct. The dog's instinct is to eliminate the stimulus by threatening to fight. But after centuries of domestication, most dogs choose to run away first.

Although dogs can often trot great distances, flat-out long-distance escape running is not what they are designed for (except breeds like greyhounds). Flight is possible in medium-length spurts only. After thousands of years of dependence on people, dogs are no longer in need of long-distance running to wear down prey in a pack hunt. They are rarely aerobically fit for long runs. Dogs that are ill-equipped physically or cognitively to face and fight a stimulus they feel is a threat will still attempt to escape.

But sometimes escape is not possible. What then? When undeveloped aerobic conditioning, genetic timidity, lack of socialization, little exposure to novel lifestyles, or hardwired breeding for high reactivity combine with inability to escape, fear aggression evolves. In the fear-aggressive dog's mind, the best defense is an offense in the form of a forward, fast, and frightening display of teeth, growls, and bite threats. The startled foe halts forward threatening motion. Once the threat is neutralized in movement, the fearful dog can run away or find a place to hide.

Limbic fear can result in an astonishingly rapid transformation from avoidance behavior to attack action. People often feel sorry for a fearful, shy dog and approach to comfort him. When the dog first cowers and then flies into an unexpected attack, well-meaning people freeze in surprise, and the dog sees his chance to get away. If the timid dog has no escape and is restrained or trapped, true aggression can result with injuries to anyone around him. Fear aggression can occur even in a well-socialized dog who, in his own interpretation of the scenario, has no alternative.

Dogs that have wider experience and/or bolder natural temperaments will seek flight less often and may choose to directly face a threat. If so, they might show several warning signs before actual bite contact. These warnings could include freezing (immediate cessation of movement to not appear as prey), lip curling, nose wrinkling, squinted eyes with the whites showing, flattened ears, head turned away, piloerection, stiff body, and successively louder growls. The tail may wag stiffly or not at all. Biting the air, known as an "air snap," is a serious warning. If these signals are ignored or go unobserved, defense contact bites follow and can lead to injury.

Regardless of an individual dog's methods for dealing with fearful situations, limbic brain function is instinctual, rapid, and reflexive—not reasoned through. Flight and/or fight are survival tools. They are primary emotional spurts of panic, supplied by the energy provided by the stress hormones that race through minds and muscles.

FEAR AS A SECONDARY EMOTION

According to Darwin, when fear manifests as a secondary emotion, conscious thought is processed in the cerebral cortex where higher logic dominates reaction. A well-socialized, confident, and trained dog will allow proximity of a novel sight, sound, or object, although all primitive logic has taught him to fear and escape the unknown. A dog who trusts his handler and is accustomed to tolerating new experiences will overrule his amygdala's limbic messages and bypass emotion to the cerebral cortex. New studies continue to show that dogs are able to reason on complex levels of choice—cognitive aspects that were not known during Darwin's time.

We can help a dog learn how to tap in to his cerebral cortex reasoning by socializing him as a youngster. The vital time for laying the groundwork of building tolerance for novelty is within the first twelve weeks of a puppy's life. Exposing the puppy to a large variety of new stimuli in non-traumatic ways during this peak time of brain development will prepare him to accept new stimuli when he is older.

During those first twelve weeks, the puppy has not yet learned to be afraid. Following that time, as with human children, the puppy will go through fear stages— weeks of extreme sensitivity to things he has not seen or experienced before. The fear stage weeks vary according to breed size and rate of maturity. Sensitive exposures to new experiences, scents, sights, people, and other animals should be part of every puppy's socialization to the world he will inhabit as an adult dog. The puppy will learn to trust his leader (you) and other people during this time. Your reliable and consistent guidance through his fear stages will reap huge paybacks when the dog matures.

A dog that has been raised from puppyhood to trust human handling will not bite the first time a person hurts him. He will tolerate pain, inoculations, and other invasions of his body because he has learned to trust. Although pain-induced fear aggression is a common problem in dogs, it can be avoided when a dog is socialized and handled properly early, and for the majority of his life.

If the first twelve weeks of socialization are missed or mishandled, you will have a difficult, if not impossible, time helping an older fearful dog catch up. An older dog that is hardwired (genetically predisposed) to be reactive and sensitive to novel experiences, such as pain, will be more of a challenge. It will take longer to assist him in the development of cerebral cortex reasoning. Behavior modification programs will have to be developed and implemented slowly to help desensitize the mature dog to fearful and/or novel stimuli.

If a dog has a conditioned fear response based on previous negative experiences, skilled behavior modification will help the dog replace his conditioned fear response with more reasoned tolerance to what was once frightening. The younger the fearful pup is when behavior modification begins, the better. Also, the smaller the fright the pet experienced when he first learned to fear, the faster and more completely he will habituate to that same stimulus. A program of habituation and desensitization will move forward more slowly and may result in less success when the dog is older and/or the fear is more intense.

Sometimes fears can be lessened but not completely eliminated. But helping a mature dog learn to think through fear is possible. In this way, fear can be managed, even if it is not eliminated.

Dogs can be taught to think before they act. A dog's behavior can become flexible and his reactions variable, as the dog reasons through his predicament. The challenge in working with a fearful dog is to build trust between him and you and to allow the time for trust to override the strength of survival instincts that remain in all dogs.

Teaching a dog coping skills is a complex process but worth the effort. A dog who accomplishes such change in behavior will feel empowered by the support he receives from you, and he will gain self-confidence in judging his environment. With time, the dog will calm himself, learn to investigate feared stimuli, and determine whether any, or how much, reaction is needed for perceived survival.

When fearful dogs are successful in transferring themselves from primitive reactions to reasoned and controlled responses, they become more adaptable and therefore, more adoptable. Rehabilitators of fearful dogs are capable of saving dog lives and can take pride in the realization that the dog's life will not only be saved, but that life will be more comfortable, peaceful, and rich.

CHAPTER 2

━╱╲━

Rescued! Now What?

W hen a dog finds herself alone in the world with no one to protect and guide her, life can be a mass of overwhelming chaos. Dogs who are abandoned, isolated, or ignored face psychological trauma that can be worse than physical trauma. If they are lucky, these rejected dogs may end up in a rescue organization where they are cared about. From there, these wayward dogs have possibilities for adoptions and promising futures, or at least safe havens where their physical and emotional needs are provided for.

THE STRUCTURES OF RESCUE ORGANIZATIONS

Dogs may become homeless when they are voluntarily relinquished by their owners, become lost or abandoned, or are rescued from undesirable situations. There are four primary structures to the organizations that will accept homeless dogs: the rescue, the shelter, the municipal pound, and the sanctuary.

Rescues

Rescues are usually small, privately owned, loosely operated groups of people who share a specific common interest. For example, there are breed-specific dog rescues, cat, bird, and horse rescues. Most do not own physical structures or buildings, with the exception of horse rescues. Most rescues depend on volunteers to foster pets in their own homes until they are adopted. Some rescues receive funding from nongovernmental organizations and/or individuals. They may have regulatory 501(c)(3) designations, which makes donations to them tax deductible to the giver. Many do not have this designation and depend on volunteers to give money as well as time. Few euthanize except when dogs have extreme aggression or health issues.

Shelters

Shelters have their own buildings, almost always have 501(c)(3) designations as nonprofit organizations, and use paid staff as well as volunteers. They are usually larger than rescues and most often, they are incorporated and governed by a board of directors. They may take specific species or many species.

Like rescues, shelters hope to adopt out their animals, but too often, they must euthanize some of them because they lack funding for resources and/or space. These shelters are known as "kill" or "open-admission" shelters. They will accept any homeless animal because there is rotation in space due to euthanasia and adoption. There are "no-kill" shelters, but they are "closed-admission" facilities. They only euthanize animals with extreme health issues, which sometimes results in their inability to accept all needy pets due to lack of space and resources. With ongoing progress in the animal welfare world, there are a handful of open admission shelters that obtain such high adoption rates that they reach a no-kill level of operation.

City or Municipal Pounds

City or municipal pounds are funded by those governmental entities and take in lost and found pets, pets confiscated by animal control officers for illegal cruelty, neglect, and/or abuse, and voluntary owner relinquishments. They are open admission, but pets have finite amounts of time in these facilities. Until recently, pounds were not concerned with adoption. They simply served as a holding facility for lost animals until their owners claimed them, which, unfortunately, was a rare occurrence. At the end of the time assigned, they were euthanized to make room for incoming animals. In larger urban areas, city pounds now often transfer the most adoptable unclaimed pets to private shelters, giving them additional time for staff to find placement homes.

Sanctuaries

Sanctuaries are private or public nonprofits governed by boards of directors and funded by tax-deductible donations. They take in and keep pets for the duration of their lives, regardless of adoptability, health, or behavioral issues. Because sanctuaries receive many unadoptable pets, the ensuing expenses can be high, especially if pets are elderly, ill, or require special facilities for safekeeping (as in court-ordered aggression cases). They will engage in humane euthanasia when the established criterion for quality of life is breached. Sanctuaries are expensive to run and are the least numerous and most short-lived of all the rescue organizations.

The animal welfare profession has increased animal cognitive and emotional research. This has resulted in greater awareness of the necessity for enrichment in captive environments and in animals' relationships with handlers in those environments. Consequently, many rescues, shelters, and sanctuaries have made efforts to provide mental and physical stimulation for animals in their care. They also seek to develop relationships between caregivers and their animals.

THE CASE FOR RELATIONSHIP BUILDING WITH FEARFUL HOMELESS DOGS

To their credit, more rescue organizations are developing and incorporating programs that address fear and insecurity in the dogs they provide safe haven for. They seek to take the edge off minor fears caused by new environments with new companions and they strive to help dogs settle in to their temporary homes at the facility. Unfortunately, these programs meet with mixed success.

The problem with these programs is that they do not have the staff or time to alleviate severe fear issues for animals that are genetically or behaviorally prone to insecurity. Some dogs are bred with natural hardwiring that makes them skittish and overreactive. Some of them come from neglectful or abusive backgrounds that have altered whatever natural hardwiring they were born with, even if they were not originally fear prone.

NATURE VS. NURTURE IN FEAR DEVELOPMENT

Studies have shown that environments and treatment (nurture) can alter innate hardwiring (nature). In one study with rats, a fearful and reactive mother rat was given the pups of a calm, easygoing mother and hers were traded to a high-strung mother. When all the babies had grown to adulthood, the originally calm baby mice had become like their adoptive mother—hypervigilant and fearful of new stimuli. The genetically reactive babies that were raised by the caring, calm mother had become like her—confident and more apt to boldly explore new environments.

Other studies with human adopted children showed that their hardwiring (personality traits from the natural parents) remained, regardless of the adoptive parents' personalities. Some tempering of sociability was observed in the adopted children, but the true character of the children (nature) overcame the adoptive parents' temperamental influence (nurture) as the children's personalities evolved.

The conclusion seems to be that inborn temperament can be influenced by environment to a great degree but brain function is largely inherited. Brain chemistry cannot be controlled—whether by a dog or by a person— without much guidance, practice, and possibly, drug therapy.

Occasionally, pharmacological intervention helps control dog brain chemistry. Antianxiety and antidepressant drugs that work for people often help regulate a dog's brain chemistry as well. And while fearful dogs are the largest challenge for rescue staff, most rescue organizations do not have access to or finances for these therapies, let alone staff experienced enough to develop and administer a pharmacological program for fearful dogs. They must deal with the resources they have and try to determine how to best address dog anxiety through environmental and behavioral approaches.

WHY SHELTER BEHAVIOR MODIFICATION PROGRAMS MAY NOT WORK

Unable to move, the terrier-mix dog froze in her fetal position in the corner of the cage. She had been curled up in a tight ball since her arrival at the shelter. Immobilized with fear, the matted, muddy, emaciated dog lay with her eyes shut in a mental state of shutdown and helplessness.

Past cruel treatment and neglectful environments can override a dog's natural temperament, particularly if she has suffered long-term mistreatment, which can present as post-traumatic stress disorder (PTSD). If the dog has never known kind treatment, she has no memory of kindness. Regardless of the benevolent treatment dogs may find in a rescue facility, they will continue the only reactive behavior they know. They must be methodically taught better ways of coping. Unfortunately, comprehensive behavior modification programs often take more time than staff and the facility can provide. Also, the number of dogs in need can overtake facility resources—both financially and physically.

When shelters enroll dogs in confidence-building or fear-desensitization programs, the dogs have only days or weeks of behavior modification, and these programs are usually class-like in nature and done in training rooms or similar venues. The problems with these approaches are numerous.

Not Enough Time for Relationship Building

Each dog has a finite amount of time with a trainer she does not know and may never see outside the classroom. From the dog's experience, people come and go, which makes trust and relaxation difficult. The animal has learned to self-protect both physically and emotionally, so brief encounters with a compassionate trainer will have little lasting effect on behavior that has been ingrained over the dog's entire life or has been traumatically inflicted.

Inadequate Consistency in Trainers and Techniques

Different trainers may work with the dog on assigned days and hours. Despite rigorous regulations in protocols, trainers vary in their techniques. Voice, touch, scent, and movement differences between people are unique, so each session the dog must spend precious time attempting to learn new "language" during her time with each new trainer. This makes progress slow because the trainer cannot start from the last leave-off point of the previous trainer. They must allow the dog adjustment time, review previous desensitization exercises, and then slowly advance with exposure to fear stimuli.

Unfamiliar Locations

Dogs quickly learn that humans enter their kennel with requirements. People do not typically have time to sit quietly in a kennel or allow a timid dog time to approach them. They enter the dog's enclosure, put on a leash, or bodily pick up the dog and transport her to the training area, which is a new environment.

The dog may have come to feel her kennel is a "safe place," but the training room is another area with new sights, sounds, smells, lighting, substrate, air temperature, and circulation—all of which she is alert and sensitive to. Consequently, the dog may become conflicted about the training session. She may look forward to the companionship of a kind person to break the monotony of her kennel but also dread the confusing interactions people will demand of her in another locale.

Previously Learned Anxiety

The dog's struggles to understand may be exacerbated by learned anxiety stemming from the emotional, verbal, and/or physical punishment she received from previous owners when she failed to understand their demands on her. This conflict of emotion produces stress for a dog who already has compromised ability to cope with novelty.

Difficulty in Identifying Fear Triggers

Figuring out what a dog is afraid of can be a laborious, time-consuming task. Often, dogs base fears on episodes of exposure that no temporary trainer in an enclosed room can be aware of. One good example comes from Temple Grandin, a famous animal behaviorist and stock facility designer. Temple was trying to determine why cattle on a ranch would not enter a loading chute. She bent down to their visual level and, through the chute railings, saw a ranch hand's yellow rain slicker draped over a fence post. Based on her knowledge of cow behavior, she conjectured that as it blew in the breeze, that strange sight caused the first cow in the line to balk, which then prevented the entire herd from progressing up the chute ramp. None of the ranch hands who worked with the cattle daily were able to think like a cow and no one had bothered to climb into the chute and look around. Once the cause of the fear was determined, the problem could be solved.

Unless the trainer has experience working with the kind of fear that has traumatized a dog in training, the fear stimuli may not be identified and addressed. Even if the specific trigger is identified, shelters do not have the time and resources to expose timid pets to common home-based fear triggers such as vacuum cleaners, umbrellas, thunder, or any of the other stimuli that can cause an unsure pet anxiety.

Some dogs learn to associate unrelated stimuli and cognitively pair them, resulting in one trigger that causes a fearful response. For example, a dog on a walk with her owner in a residential neighborhood shies from a trashcan on the curb, then cautiously approaches it to investigate. At the exact moment the dog's nose comes in contact with the plastic can, a car down the street backfires, which sends the dog into panicked escape behavior.

From then on, the dog may be afraid of trash cans (or perhaps anything plastic) because she has no way of knowing the sound was not related to her approach to and/or touch of the trash can. The owner will not know what caused the extreme reaction. Perhaps the human was not focused on the dog when the incident happened and did not see the dog touch the trash can. All the owner saw was a startled dog. Even if the owner did see the dog touch the can, he might not have made the connection because humans filter out unrelated stimuli due to our own socialization and experiences.

As a species, we are not as fearful of sudden, novel sounds as other animals are. We can also logically identify the sounds that animals cannot. While a human can identify the sound of a backfiring car, a dog will probably not have an earlier experience to associate it with. It will take an extremely aware and knowledgeable handler to eventually figure out and connect the two fear stimuli that have now become one in the dog's mind. This scenario cannot be discovered or replicated in a training room.

Maintenance Reinforcement Is Lacking

When the assigned time for a shelter dog's behavior modification is ended, either for the day or for the rest of the dog's stay in the rescue environment, whatever progress has been made will disappear if conscientious effort is not made to continually reinforce the new learning.

In many shelters, dogs are allowed perhaps six confidence-building sessions and then are left in their kennels to await adoption. Dogs do not generalize new knowledge well. For instance, if you teach a dog to sit in the dining room, that training does not easily generalize to sitting elsewhere, such as the kitchen. She must be retrained until she knows that "sit" means the same thing wherever she is. In the same way, whatever the dog learned during her sessions in the training facility will not transfer to a new home with a new owner. She will have to be retrained.

Facility training problems can be addressed when the fearful dog is placed in a foster home where an experienced caregiver can provide individualized and consistent methods of habituation and desensitization in a calmer environment.

THE ADVANTAGE OF FOSTER HOMES

For the first time in her two-year life, the terrier was not hit, yelled at, or chained. She did not have to compete with other dogs to fill her stomach. She was bathed, brushed, trimmed, and loved. She had a clean house, yard, and bed. When new people visited she learned to trust and know that the woman who cared for her would not allow anyone to hurt her.

All dogs need an ongoing relationship with their people and routine in their lifestyles, which are next to impossible in a shelter kennel facility. A sense of safety and trust will develop with daily structure, the presence of the same handler, a familiar environment, and time to learn. Many timid dogs will voluntarily seek out safe places such as the corner of a couch, a specific stair, or a cave-like space under a piece of furniture, none of which are available in facility kennels. The dog must be physically and emotionally comfortable in order to develop emotional trust and learn intellectual coping skills.

Behavior modification programs must be designed for each dog's needs, and they must be implemented in small increments towards the future goal of a life without fear. A foster caregiver can provide more one-on-one attention and monitoring than shelter staff. When fear is lessened and trust is established, the first steps towards a true relationship between the dog and caregiver can begin. Most dogs are cognitively predestined to attach themselves to their "pack" members. When a dog accepts the person they live with as a family pack member, an attachment is forged that may supersede previous learned behaviors. Even some hardwired reactions will become less severe if the dog sees no need for them in her current life.

More shelters are turning to foster volunteers for assistance with their dogs who do not cope well in an institutionalized setting. Fostering saves countless dog's lives. Dogs whose personalities are shut down in shelters commonly come to life in their temporary homes.

CHAPTER 3

-/|\-

Beginning Rehabilitation
with a Fearful Dog

*B*ailey, a two-year-old Wheaten Terrier, was relinquished to a large city shelter by the family she lived with for almost two years. She had spent the first four months of her life in a pet store cage after being bred in yet a smaller cage at a Midwest puppy mill. She and her two siblings were taken from their mother at six weeks of age instead of the recommended eight weeks. They were trucked across country in a rickety van filled with stinking kennels of puppies in the same plight. By the time Bailey arrived at the pet store that had purchased her, she had lost her mother, siblings, and the only world she knew.

High-strung and nervous, Bailey had not eaten during the trip and was depressed and weak upon her arrival. Once placed in the pet store cage, she ate sparingly and whined incessantly. That is where the newlyweds spotted her on a Sunday stroll through the mall. The wife begged her husband to buy Bailey, and so she entered her first real home.

Bailey's new home was a neat and sparsely furnished apartment where she was left alone during the day while the couple worked. Confined to the kitchen, Bailey had pee pads, toys, water, a bed, and puppy food. When the couple returned in the evenings, she was coddled and cuddled. She learned to walk on a leash and loved exploring outside with her people. Bailey relaxed into her new life.

One year later, Bailey's owners had a baby, a colicky child who screamed at all hours. The parents got by with little sleep, and the wife stayed home to tend to the sick baby. Bailey did not get as many walks. In fact, she rarely got any exercise. Her puppy energy built up and manifested in nervous behaviors such as restless pacing of the two-bedroom apartment. When the child began to crawl, the family moved to a bigger house. The change unnerved Bailey. Unfamiliar furniture was added and her puppy bed was replaced with a new adult one. Bailey's exhausted mistress barely spent any time with her, so she was on her own to figure out appropriate reactions to an animated, arm waving creature who could emit vocal pitches that nearly broke Bailey's eardrums.

Physically and emotionally sensitive to fast movements, high-pitched squeals, and enthusiastic infant approaches, Bailey began to growl at the toddler whenever he waddled towards her. She sought resting areas away from the intruder, but to no avail. Fascinated by Bailey's soft fluffy hair, the child never ceased to grab and pull until Bailey cried. The baby also sometimes pounded her with his chubby but club-like fists. Bailey gave many dog warnings but no one noticed or understood. One day she nipped the baby's hand when he reached for her.

Aghast, the young mother swooped in and removed the child, then scolded Bailey when she returned. By that time

Bailey only knew she had succeeded in having the child removed and had no idea why her mistress yelled at her. She slinked away to her favorite corner of the couch, her "safe place," until the child grew tall enough to reach her.

Twice more the incident was repeated with toddler attempts to corner the dog. Bailey exhibited the only warning she knew they would pay attention to. The evening she snapped at the baby in front of the father was her last night in her home.

The next morning, the man took Bailey to the shelter and filled out a questionnaire listing reasons for her relinquishment. "We want to have a baby and so must get rid of the dog," he wrote. "She is a wonderful pet, loves car rides, and has a sweet personality." He did not add that they already were parents, or that Bailey was child-aggressive because she had not been carefully habituated to children, which had further exacerbated her insecurity. He also neglected to say that she had come from a pet store where she had been caged during her crucial brain development and socialization months and had never been out of either of their homes, except for occasional walks, which were recently discontinued.

Placed alone in a kennel to await behavior and health evaluations by shelter staff, Bailey became emotionally catatonic. She shut down from overwhelming confusion, fear, and inability to cope with the upheaval in her life. She refused to eat or drink, curled into a ball on the cold concrete floor, then urinated and defecated where she lay. The behavior employee who came to evaluate her could not get Bailey to rouse, and so she was scheduled for euthanasia due to extreme fear.

The day before her appointment with death, a kind woman in the foster care department called a volunteer who specialized in fearful dogs. When Bailey refused to unwrap herself from her balled up posture, the reeking, filthy dog was forcibly but gently carried out. The instant she saw the open car door, Bailey flew out of the woman's arms and into the backseat. On the ride to her foster home, Bailey watched the scenery speed by with anxiety but interest.

Bailey became a real dog again as she walked on a leash in her new yard. She was fascinated by scents, played with balls, and interacted with her caregiver affectionately. However, during her first two weeks in foster care, Bailey's anxiety caused diarrhea, vomiting, and uncontrolled urination. The foster home was set up for easy dog cleanups and Bailey was never chastised for behavior she could not control.

Bailey spent three months in her foster home. There she learned a strict daily dog regimen. She regained control of her bodily functions, and with daily physical exercise, her temperament began to calm. Underneath her insecurity, the foster volunteer found a dog eager to understand and please.

Training in household manners and basic obedience progressed well. Bailey loved to learn and earn praise, but her lack of security "in case" she made a mistake in behavior still caused hesitancy in her performance. This slowness to respond with confidence was ignored, rather than criticized, and when she did execute the behavior requested, Bailey received abundant praise in forms she could deal with: quiet but happy verbal commendation, affectionate and gentle physical contact. On occasion, food treats were offered, but Bailey was not a highly food motivated dog and rejected food when under stress. However, she did respond well to physical affection and verbal praise.

Bailey was adopted by a middle-aged couple who passed the criteria required by the shelter, and she entered her third home. The new mistress was kind and attentive, and at first, Bailey settled in well. The new home routine was purposely set up to mimic the one at her foster home, so she tolerated the change reasonably well, despite her naturally high-strung personality.

One night, the husband returned home drunk and a raucous battle between him and his soft-spoken wife ensued. When he struck his wife, Bailey broke into a cacophony of barks to protect the woman who had been kind to her. Her protection frightened the man and he left the house. Confused and anxious, Bailey attempted to find comfort by curling up next to the weeping woman where she had landed on the kitchen floor.

After her mistress went to bed, Bailey experienced diarrhea and vomited numerous times around the house. The man returned in the morning before the mistress rose and discovered Bailey's messes. When the man saw them, he loudly announced to his timid wife, "It's our marriage or the dog." The woman returned Bailey to the shelter in tears. In a few hours, Bailey's foster mistress came for her.

One night after returning to her foster home, Bailey courageously drove a potential intruder away from the front door when he jimmied the lock. Bailey threw herself into the door glass as she bellowed threatening vocalizations. Even after the bad man ran away, formerly timid Bailey slept in front of the door the rest of the night. Her foster mistress adopted her.

Bailey's continued behavioral evolvement was proven when she appeared in a television commercial for the shelter. She faced the film studio's strange equipment, lights, and numerous people with confidence. She calmly watched rabbits, hamsters, cats, birds, and other dogs romp around the filming area and obediently looked to her mistress for performance hand signals.

Seven years later, Bailey is a different dog. She greets strangers on walks, travels to new environments, no longer growls at children, and uses her safe places in the house less frequently. She is bonded to another dog in the family who came after her. She tolerates exposure to unfamiliar dogs, people, and places with equanimity.

Bailey has a large yard to play in and is walked every day. She no longer reacts to prior fear stimuli such as black coats, tall people, big purses, dropped items, or high-pitched noises. People who knew her when she first came to her mistress's home cannot believe she is the same dog.

But the final proof that Bailey had risen above her early traumas occurred in her sixth year when she approached and gently took a treat offered from a three-year-old toddler's outstretched palm.

HOW TO BEGIN REHABILITATION

How did Bailey's foster caregiver/new owner accomplish such change in the dog? When Bailey arrived, she was provided with a calm and quiet environment to help her decompress. When her diarrhea and vomiting subsided and she slept through the night without whining, exercise regimens were developed. They consisted of long walks at the same time every day with another dog she learned to trust and depend on and play in the backyard in the morning and afternoon. Bailey's walks were directed toward physical exercise only. She was led away from any stress producing stimuli such as children's playgrounds.

Although early on, Bailey's foster caregiver did not know about her fear aggression towards children, she avoided playgrounds because she knew most dogs, especially skittish ones, are uncomfortable around rambunctious children.

Bailey's time in the yard was confined behind a six-foot wooden privacy fence so outside fear producing stimuli, such as dog and human passersby were not visible. The dissipation of energy made possible by freedom in the backyard resulted in physical and emotional stress reduction. With healthy outlets, Bailey became calmer and better able to deal with novelty in her life.

Evenings were spent in the family room with innocuous, nonviolent, soft television because the caregiver knew that dogs can be aroused by violence and human anger on the television, just as in the reality of their home. Days consisted of ongoing classical music. Meals were free-fed, which supported her naturally slow eating habits and prevented her anxiety from interfering with her digestion, and allowed her colon to settle. She had regular trips to the yard for urination and defecation and was taught words for each so when the door opened on a snowy day or night, she knew what was expected. Bailey was able to choose her resting areas and when she retreated to her safe places—on the couch or a particular stair—no one touched her until she came forward on her own.

After her return from the unsettling experience of her adoption, the previous routines were reestablished and Bailey resettled more quickly than the first time. Then she was able to continue to learn how to process and cope with novel stimuli. Bailey's former foster caregiver/new owner consulted with her knowledgeable veterinarian and both agreed that Bailey would benefit from a mild antianxiety medication. When therapeutic levels were reached, Bailey was introduced to her owner's relatives, two toddlers. The children were educated on Bailey's needs, and although very young, they were sensitive to Bailey's insecurities and eager to help her. The dog ceased her fear-aggressive displays. She learned that the noise and activity level of small children was not threatening and that she had the option of removing herself from them whenever she had enough. The children understood when Bailey left on a voluntary "time out" and they left her alone.

With the help of medication and skillful behavior modification, Bailey's limbic fear dissipated and she was able to learn. She learned to evaluate each situation and determine how to react. Because praise always accompanied correct decisions, she finally found her life less confusing. Bailey still had off days when her anxiety escalated to some degree, but she had the coping skills and the support of a calm, nonjudgmental, nonpunitive owner to help her through.

DEPARTURES FROM ROUTINE

Structure in a fearful dog's life is crucial to the establishment of comfort, relaxation, and anxiety relief. Only then can the animal begin to learn how to cope with her own fears. Once the dog's anxiety level is dropped, the dog can feel safe in her routine, and learning can begin. Small departures (in type, time, and intensity) from the initial routine will be less stressful because the animal understands that she can and will eventually return to that routine.

For example, if you regularly take your dog for a walk at 10:00 a.m., she will anticipate the exercise, the release of pent-up energy, the exposure to interesting activity, and upcoming companionship with you. She will return from the walk calmer and more able to learn the rest of the day's lessons because her stress hormones have been dissipated through vigorous exercise. As time with you passes, she will learn to hold her anxiety to a tolerable level because she knows a walk is coming. She will be fully capable of comprehending the positive feelings that exercise provides her, even if she cannot verbalize why she feels better afterwards. Her growing trust in your attention and her daily routine will transfer into any small departures from that routine.

To test her ability to handle a departure from a set routine, periodically randomize the time of the walk by fifteen minutes for one day. For instance, if you routinely walk her at 10:00 a.m., take her for her walk at 10:15 a.m. for one day only. Then return to the original schedule the next few days. After a few days back in her routine, wait thirty to forty minutes after 10:00 a.m. Follow that by returning to the 10:00 a.m. time for the next day or two, then take her out fifteen to thirty minutes early. Gradual departures from routine while still sticking to what she actually needs—physical dissipation of anxiety—will help the dog adjust to less rigid schedules, without causing undue stress, or overloading her with change.

SAFE PLACES

Rehabilitating a fearful dog requires that the caregiver be alert to the needs of that particular animal. Some fearful dogs need places within their environment that they consider safe and choose those places for themselves. The caregiver must be vigilant to make sure the dog is never frightened in those places. Safe places should always be respected because they are the baseline building block of a human's support, and therefore the first step in building the dog's trust. A fearful dog must be able to trust the humans around her to honor her chosen safe place.

Once a dog realizes that a small space in her world is safe, it will be easier to help her expand her perspective to gradually see larger and larger areas as nonthreatening and, therefore, not frightening. That is why fearful dogs, regardless of their size, need to be habituated to small initial areas, such as your kitchen or family room. These initial small areas should be near, or in, an active gathering place for her new family, a place where she is exposed to household commotion but with outskirt safe places where she can observe if she does not choose to participate. Giving a fearful dog full run of a house and yard before she is ready to explore on her own can be overwhelming to her. The same is true if she is thrown into family commotion with no place to remove herself if her stress level rises. Let her tell you when she is ready to reach out into new territory or to join in family action.

The availability of a safe place will provide an anxious dog with the ability to decompress. There, she can put herself into a voluntary time out. She will then begin to lose high-level reactivity to the noise, scent, and visual novelties common in human households. Once the dog's trust in you and sense of safety in her environment is built, purposeful and structured habituation to her fear triggers can begin.

DESENSITIZATION

To begin mild desensitization, feared stimuli should be introduced slowly, and never near the dog's chosen safe places. At first, fear producing sounds, smells, or visual stimuli should be used when the dog is far away from the source. The dog can be gradually brought closer to the source as she becomes familiar with and desensitized to whatever it is that makes her anxious.

For example, if the sound of a vacuum cleaner frightens the dog, start by placing the dog in the closest area to the sound that does not elicit extreme avoidance or escape behavior. When the dog becomes more accustomed and less reactive to the machine, gradual movement closer can proceed. Another possibility for helping the dog to adjust to a feared stimulus is to use a smaller version of /less intense exposure to the feared source. In the case of vacuum cleaner fear, start at a distance with a smaller, handheld model. Habituate the dog to that machine and then start over at a distance with the larger machine that will eventually be part of her life in her home.

In all desensitization efforts, you must always be careful to avoid pushing the dog into a fearful reaction or your efforts will have to be restarted from the beginning position. Also, she must have an escape route available, in case you misread what she is ready for. There is no point in forced overexposure to a fear trigger, and sometimes you will not know when that point is reached in the dog's psyche.

The idea behind desensitization is to gradually increase exposures to anything that sets off limbic fear and panic in your dog. Being sensitive to your dog's needs for support, encouragement, and carefully controlled exposure to her fear triggers will yield long-term advantages, although the initial steps may seem slow. Patience is the key and is easier to practice when you have a genuine interest in and concern for the dog you are trying to help.

THE BASIC KEY TO BEHAVIOR MODIFICATION

Your careful eye will need to be on the lookout for an escalation in reaction. If your dog begins the slightest negative reaction, exposure to the stimuli must be backed up to a previous level that causes no response in the dog, be it distance, intensity, or both.

Most importantly, distance and intensity must never be addressed together at the beginning of the behavior modification program. One hurdle must be scaled first, then the other in separate tests of exposure. Close proximity and high intensity may be paired only when consistent and reliable temperament changes are proven in the dog. With gradual exposure, myriad smells, household sounds, and common sights will become part of the dog's daily routine home experiences. Once habituated, your dog will find her home a place of safety, instead of a place of multiple scary sensory experiences.

HOW A DOG SENSES FEAR STIMULI

Dogs can be sensitive to sounds, smells, and/or movements. One or more of these can be fear triggers so as you get to know your dog, watch carefully. Try to see how she perceives her environment. You may never know what triggered her initial anxiety or how it is related to different stimuli that you, as a human, would not necessarily associate. It does not matter why your dog is afraid of something; it only matters how you deal with her in the here and now. Some approaches may include the following issues.

Sound

Sound sensitive dogs must at first be provided with smaller, quieter versions of routine home sounds. As already discussed, a small hand vacuum should be followed by the larger version at a distance, then brought slowly into the animal's presence. Laundry machines should be used behind a closed door and then the door gradually opened, farther and farther. House repair construction should be done only when the dog is gone, has a ready escape route available, or has been habituated enough to not have a negative reaction.

Dogs are more sound sensitive than cats and people, so you must pay close attention to a timid dog's status when exposed to new sounds. Throughout habituation to environmental sounds, low-level ambient auditory stimulation should be used to neutralize stress. Ambient sounds are innocuous sounds that cause no reaction in the dog and which may distract her from the intensity of a sound she is truly fearful of. The most cost-effective, easily accessible thing to create peaceful ambiance for an anxious dog is music. Studies now show that classical and easy-listening instrumental music are most effective.

Smells

Olfactory (scent) associations can trigger fear reactions in dogs. Domestic breeding has evolved a larger dependency on sight for dogs, but some breeds (hunting and scent hounds) retain hyperawareness of surrounding scents. If a dog has experienced a cruel or frightening episode and has learned (either through actual association or unrelated association) that a particular scent elicits a negative stimulus, she will react with anxiety. For minor scent reactions, antianxiety scent motivators can noticeably calm dogs. DAP (Dog Appeasing Pheromone) or similar products that contain particular pheromones can soothe a restless dog.

Scents that evoke more intense fear responses should be made note of and avoided at first. Gradually reintroduce them at distance, and then introduce them at slowly increased intensity to habituate the dog without causing a reaction. Sometimes scent reactivity is related in the dog's mind to a past fearful event, which you may never know about or be able to replicate. Scent habituation will have to be slow and accompanied by positive reinforcement, which will switch her association of the smell from something frightening to association with rewards, not the original event.

For example, if a dog was abused by a man who smoked cigarettes, the scent of cigarette smoke may set the dog off in fearful reactions. Or perhaps the dog experienced a house fire and the trauma has been deeply imprinted in her memory. If the dog is expected to be in an environment where smoke is a component or if the only goal is to remove generalized fear of smoke for the dog's own comfort in her life, exposure to mild smoke at a distance can be started. Most animals fear smoke because they innately fear fire. Do not force a dog to face dense smoke of any kind, simply for health reasons. But if you and your dog pass cigarette smokers while walking down a street and you see alarm in the dog, desensitization is certainly in order. The goal is always to provide the dog with a learned ability to deal with normal, common life stimuli without alarm or insecurity.

Movement

Sudden movement will also cause fear reactions in dogs. Dogs will often miss movement at a distance that their taller human companions easily see because dogs are primarily scenting animals and keep their heads to the ground, sniffing. Despite differences in breed and height, all dogs learn about their close environment by smelling, and so are primarily focused on what is in their immediate vicinity. If a dog with a fragile temperament raises his head from a focused scent and suddenly becomes aware of something moving nearby, he can panic.

Also, because of years of evolving safely in domesticity, most dogs have lost the primitive fears once needed to ensure their survival, and therefore have lost the hypervigilance that less domesticated animals or prey-like animals (like pet birds, cats, and horses) still possess. But genetically reactive and fearful dogs seem to retain much of the hypervigilance seen in prey species.

Sensitive dogs often display hypervigilance and they may show fears that seem to you to be illogical and possibly silly. These temperamental dogs may show anxiety around moving human feet, hands, eyes, facial expressions, straight-on body postures, leaning forward, crouching, or even rising from a chair. They may also panic at flapping material, wind in trees, strobing lights, and shuddering shadows. When they see movement they have no experience with, reactive dogs are hard wired to run away first and think later.

DISCOVERING FEAR TRIGGERS AND PROVIDING ESCAPE

All fearful dogs must be given a means of escape from that which frightens them, so they have power over the speed, intensity, and proximity of their own exposure. This is especially true during the initial evaluation phase of rehabilitation when you have not fully discovered the dog's fear triggers. The escape must be into a controlled and safe area. There the dog can return to neutral emotion without being reinforced by complete avoidance, such as running far away from whatever frightened her. Escape routes allow the animal to lower her own fear responses. Stress hormones can then dissipate and she can reenter the realm of reasoning. Dog doors, separate rooms, or highly fenced areas should be available as the dog learns that flight is not necessary. Because her escape route gave her the ability to get to a safe distance without complete escape, she will probably return to investigate the feared object or person. Fearful animals are often the most curious, once their fear calms.

However, without an escape route, fear aggression may result. If the dog sees no other alternative to solve her fear, she may react aggressively to achieve distance between herself and whatever or whoever is scaring her.

Successful fear aggression will become a self-reinforcing behavior. For example, surprise aggression from a timid dog will certainly stop the approach of a feared person. Once a dog learns that aggressive posturing stops or drives away the frightening stimuli, she will quickly resort to the tactic again. Fear aggression has been shown to increase in intensity with each successful manifestation, so avoiding it to begin with is the most desirable and practical approach. You must make sure that fear aggression is not a successful resort of choice for your fearful dog. Providing an escape route is key to giving the frightened dog a sense of control over her situation.

When the dog chooses to escape to a distance where she feels safe, your response should never be negative, corrective, or loud. Calm, ongoing activity in the area that startled her should be carried on and only quiet calming tones of voice should be used around her. Do not try to touch, catch, or hold the dog while she is severely frightened. She may interpret your contact as restraint, rather than comfort. You might place yourself in a dangerous position if she has not returned to a calmer state of mind.

Your dog will learn to observe your own reaction to what frightened her. If she sees no panic in you, she will process the lack of reaction in her "leader" and calm herself. If there is another resident dog who is less reactive, the fearful dog will absorb the behavior of the "leader dog" before depending on a human guide. Dogs do learn from observing others they trust—peer dogs first, then people.

The timid dog must be allowed to return on her own, without force. When she does investigate the feared object she must receive gentle positive reinforcement, even if her return is initially at a distance. Her return and willing approach illustrates the dog's passing from primitive limbic fear to cerebral cortex reasoning on her own—a key sign of success in rehabilitation.

Your ultimate goal is to make the dog's emotional need to escape unnecessary. You must be constantly vigilant in your awareness of how your pet may see, hear, and smell her surroundings. Thinking like a dog is the key to preemptive interference of negative responses. The ideal scenario is to provide the fearful dog with a proper habituation and desensitization routine that negates the necessity for fear in the first place. Never push a fearful animal over her tolerance threshold or it will become necessary to back up in the whole process, perhaps even to the beginning.

Forcing a dog to face her fears will backfire. Pushing a dog towards panic will result only in her increased fear of you, someone she should be able to count on as a friend and protector. When she loses faith in your support, she may enter a realm of deeper fear, uncontrollable panic, and more severe psychological damage. She will then enter the limbic reaction of "going over threshold."

-,ı\-

Over Threshold

Shadow, a three-year-old Australian Shepherd had been recently adopted from a shelter. The veterinarian had told Shadow's new owner that the shepherd needed a blood test for heartworms. If the test was negative, heartworm medication would be necessary through the summer mosquito season. Shadow's owner made an appointment.

When they arrived at the veterinary clinic, Shadow manifested fearful body posture, and although he was large for his breed, Shadow tried to hide under his owner's chair in the waiting room. Once escorted into the exam room, the vet entered, bent over the dog, reached out, scooped him up in his arms, and plopped him onto a metal examination table. Further unnerved by the vet's aggressive approach and overpowering physical dominance of him, Shadow became more insecure and leaned against his owner for comfort as she stood on the opposite side of the examination table.

A technician entered and grabbed the dog in a tight hold, placing herself between the dog and his trusted new owner. The vet switched on buzzing clippers and shaved Shadow's neck. Shadow startled when the vibration on his throat cut through to his naked skin. The vet inserted a needle in an attempt to find his jugular vein. Fear, pain, insecurity, and apparent lack of support and protection by his owner sent Shadow into panic. He wriggled, whined, and tried to back away from the repeated attempts by the vet to find his vein with several sticks. Shadow could not get away from the pain and the aggressive humans, so finally he bared his teeth. Nobody noticed.

Shadow scrambled backwards and almost fell off the table. Grabbed again, the vet lost patience and yelled at Shadow to hold still. The wrestling match became a full-blown pain-induced fear aggression display as the frightened dog flailed, whined, and growled. The hold on him tightened and he gasped for oxygen. Blindly, he tossed his head back and forth to get more air.

"Don't let him get away with that!" the vet yelled at the tech. Seeing that the owner was visibly upset, the vet said, "We have to teach him who's boss."

The owner had no idea how to be an advocate for her dog and assumed the vet was the professional in handling dogs.

Shadow continued to struggle, growl, and cry. When he escalated to an air snap, the noise of his teeth clashing together made everyone freeze. He had succeeded in stopping their attack on him.

OVER THRESHOLD

"Over threshold" is the term used when an animal is purposely or accidentally forced to face a stimulus that brings about panic and the nonrational, knee-jerk desire for escape from an extremely uncomfortable situation. Over threshold means that the animal has lost control of logic and his brain is engulfed with stress hormones, making reasoned thought or learning impossible. The only reaction the animal can muster is to get away, whether that is accomplished by running away or fighting his way out of the immense discomfort he is in.

If the dog has an escape route, he will try to run. If he does not have one, he may try to fight his way to freedom. An experienced handler may see a dog's gradual build-up to panic, with accompanying dog warnings, but this intense change in behavior can also happen in an instant, without noticeable warnings.

PURPOSEFUL FLOODING

One way to throw a fearful animal over threshold is flooding. Flooding can be purposeful intense exposure of an animal to fear stimuli with the hope that the animal will become overwhelmed and cease to react, also known as "shutdown" or "learned helplessness."

Learned Helplessness: A Rat's Story

Learned helplessness was first discovered accidentally when scientists studied operant conditioning (causing an animal to associate positives and negatives with rewards or punishments). A laboratory rat was placed in a two-sided cage. On both ends of the cage were levers that could dispense rewarding food pellets. The researchers "loaded" a sound cue, such as a bell, by teaching the rat that when the bell rang, food would appear on one side of the cage. Then they taught the rat that it must depress the lever so the food would drop down into its bowl.

When they rang the bell, the rat ran over to the lever and pushed. Food appeared. After the rat conquered that learning, the researchers taught it that the same thing would happen on the opposite side of the cage with the lever located there. Once the rat reliably ran from one lever to the other to obtain food, the researchers placed a mechanism that would give an electric shock to the rat when it ran to one of the sides previously dispensing food.

At the ring of the bell, the conditioned rat ran to get food, but instead of receiving food, received a shock. Confused, the rat ran to the opposite side, where it did receive food. The rat quickly became trained to leave the bad side of the cage and go to the good side to avoid the shock and to obtain food.

Then the researchers switched sides with the food and the shocking device. After initial fear and confusion, the rat learned to also switch sides for its reward of a food pellet. At that time, the researchers changed the operation again so that the rat received a shock instead of food on both sides of the cage. Ever the optimist, the poor rat ran back and forth trying to obtain food but received only shocks.

Finally it gave up. It retreated to the center of the cage and would not move. It had learned that only negative and painful consequences were the results of anything it did, so it shut down. It lay in the center of the cage, apparently resigned to whatever terrible fate would befall it. This was the discovery of learned helplessness. Without the ability to earn a positive reward or escape pain, the rat ceased to react to anything. It became catatonic.

CATATONIC BEHAVIOR

Catatonic behavior can result when any animal feels hopelessness in his situation. Catatonic behavior may manifest in body postures such as curling into a ball, averted or closed eyes, lying splayed out, and/or complete immobility. Facial expression becomes blank or often sorrowful, and the animal will refuse to interact. Catatonic learned helplessness is a serious condition from which the animal may never recover. It is an example of post-traumatic stress disorder (PTSD) that can be found in dogs.

Yet some people believe that the complete shutdown of the animal proves it has become accustomed to the stimulus. In reality, it has not become desensitized, it has experienced severe mental damage. Intelligent, highly social animals like dogs are particularly prone to emotional and cognitive impairment under duress. Flooding has no scientific or moral place in desensitization and habituation programs.

FEAR AGGRESSION

The opposite of immobile, catatonic shutdown is active fear aggression. Fear aggression begins when a dog sees no other way out of a desperately frightening situation in which he feels trapped and completely overwhelmed.

Over-the-top forced exposure to fear is flooding, and this frequently results in a dog who feels that aggression is his only resort to escape an intolerable situation. A dog who succeeds in eliminating his exposure to a feared stimulus by aggressive behavior (for instance, by causing the human to withdraw) is automatically reinforced and that behavior will continue, often escalating with each new success in avoidance.

Pain is an obvious motivation for avoidance behavior. When a dog sees no way to escape a human source of pain, such as needed veterinary care, he will protect himself by attacking, regardless of his previous experiences with people. It is difficult to determine each dog's limits for pain tolerance. For some it may be inoculations; for others, broken bones. If you carefully observe your dog's facial expression and body language, you may be able to see his fear escalation. Knowing your dog's methods of communicating with you can help you see when he is approaching his breaking point.

If you feel and see his tolerance waning, cease all threatening interaction. If medical care is urgent he should be sedated, rather than allow him to go over threshold and into pain-induced fear aggression. Once pain-induced fear aggression becomes a habit, it will escalate and will be extremely difficult to eliminate.

Unfortunately, habitual fear aggressive dogs are not good adoption candidates and are the first to be euthanized due to the extensive and prolonged behavior modification that is required to teach more acceptable behavior alternatives to stress, if indeed it is possible. A dog that has been inhumanely flooded has little chance of finding someone who will understand and work with him. Even if skilled behaviorists can and will work with such dogs, some dogs remain so psychologically damaged that euthanasia is the most humane option.

Attempting to place severely traumatized and/or mentally ill dogs in the community is an ongoing challenge in ethics for all rescues and shelters. Damaged dogs can remain unacceptably dangerous to the average adopter. Shelter adoption staffs are often put in the painful positions of choosing which dogs will fit into human society and which will not. People who work with dogs also suffer from psychological stress when their goal is to save dogs, but in some instances, they cannot. For these reasons, it can be said that flooding a fearful dog is always dangerous. It is inhumane and cruel—to the dog, but also to subsequent well-intentioned humans who come in contact with the unfortunate animal.

However, flooding continues to be used by ignorant or lazy handlers. Instead of slowly accustoming the dog to a feared stimulus, insensitive and/or ignorant handlers will force dogs to deal with prolonged exposure to intense fear triggers. Regardless of the dog's struggles to escape, he is held firm. Obvious failure with this approach is often ignored and handlers continue or repeat forced exposure in efforts to stop reaction. Eventually, any dog, submissive or aggressive, will cease reacting. But by this time, so much physical, emotional, and cognitive damage has occurred that the dog is completely broken down into catatonic stupor.

Even if the dog comes out of the stupor, he will never fully trust and will be fated to live a life of constant mental trauma and emotional conflict when handled by people. Plus, all other handling will likely result in additional battles. In contrast, dogs gentled into trusting their person will eventually continue to trust when asked for new levels of tolerance in handling.

In Shadow's case, his compassionate owner followed her instincts and sense of outrage at the mistreatment of her dog. She found a new veterinarian and hired an animal behaviorist to teach her how to help her dog over his new aggression "problem." She faithfully employed a long-term behavior modification program of short and positive experiences with veterinarians. Shadow gradually allowed medical handling. The owner's wise decision and compassionate care was prophetic, because Shadow was diagnosed with cancer at the age of six. He compliantly let doctors, technicians, and his loving owner nurse him until died.

ACCIDENTAL FLOODING

There are times when flooding is accidental. When you do not know a dog's history, you may inadvertently expose the dog to a stimulus that causes a mental flashback to a previous fear memory. The dog may or may not demonstrate gradually increased discomfort with continued exposure. He may transition from calm to frantic in a flash, depending on how intense his fear memory is. When you see a dog going over threshold, all exposure to the fear stimulus should halt immediately. The dog should be removed from proximity to the stimulus and calmed. This can mean that all forward progress in training up to the point of the panic may have been erased, in which case the training will need to be restarted and developed more slowly.

HUMAN FLOODING RESPONSE VS. DOG FLOODING RESPONSE

An example of human flooding was evident on the television show *Survivor*. In one episode, contestants were offered a great deal of money to allow themselves to be confined in a small space where spiders were turned loose to crawl over them. Humans have a primitive instinctual fear of spiders, so the audience was provided with a perverse form of entertainment while the contestants fought their natural instincts in favor of their greed.

When it is a choice made by the victim, flooding in the human psyche might be justifiable when money and five minutes of television fame are the reward. But fearful dogs have no ability to see such reward at the end of their experience. They see survival as their only concern. High fear reactivity in all species is based on survival instincts. But people can override their survival instincts by tapping into cerebral cortex reasoning when the possibility of achieving a goal makes it worthwhile.

Because humans can rationalize and intellectually project into the future, they are cognitively better equipped to accept flooding, if it is relatively short term and not traumatic enough to send them over their own threshold to panic. In the case of the *Survivor* contestants, this is what allowed them to override their fear of spiders for the potential monetary gain.

Dogs do not have the same cognitive ability and seem to live only in the present moment. If they can project into the future, it is a short projection. For instance, if they got a cookie the last time they sat, they may sit again based on the possibility of getting another cookie. If no reward occurs, they quickly move into another behavior. Although experts doubt that dogs have the cognitive ability to comprehend the concept of death, even the most primitive creatures possess survival instincts. Limbic or primal survival instincts will trump any other motivation for a fearful animal.

While human motivation and cognitive functioning may be more complex than dog motivation and cognitive functioning, humans and dogs are not that different at an instinctual level. Fear is uncomfortable for both humans and dogs. Lack of respect for personal space by physically forcing exposure to a fear stimulus is rude, whether it is perpetrated against a human or a dog. But with dogs, it can also become dangerous. In addition, it is counterproductive. It only results in increased fear of the stimulus and distrust of the enforcer.

Gentle, firm guidance accompanied by behavior modification is the most efficient and respectful way to deal with fears in our canine companions. When a dog is handled consistently, he will begin to open up, emotionally and cognitively, to the lessons a trusted person teaches.

~/|\~

CHAPTER 5

The Importance
of a Familiar Handler

*B*uffer *ran and ran. He ran around the huge automobile tires, past the legs of human pedestrians on the city sidewalks, and around the other dogs on leashes with their people. Buffer had no person to protect, guide, or feed him. For days he had been timidly poking through knocked over trash cans, finding tidbits in the gutters, or just going hungry. He drank sprinkler runoff water in the park. When he could find a suitable hiding place, he slept an exhausted sleep until the noise of his surroundings pierced the only peace he had been able to excape into.*

Buffer was a small buff colored terrier mix with saucer shaped brown eyes that shone with fear. His black button nose never stopped quivering as he sniffed for danger. But the world was a gigantic place for a small dog who had been dumped by people who no longer wanted him. He had never been outside the cramped and dingy apartment he was born in, so when he was dropped on the street corner in the middle of the night, he became immediately terrified of every strange scent and sight, as well as the vastness of the summer night air.

One evening, he discovered a wonderful smell and followed his nose to a bowl of mouth-watering food inside a small, dark cave amongst the shrubs in the park where he had been finding places to sleep. He approached cautiously, but his overwhelming hunger soon forced him to let down his guard and enter the cave. Before he could close his tiny drooling mouth on his first bite, a door behind him banged shut. Trapped! Buffer's appetite disappeared in his frenzied battle against the steel bars of the cave, which was actually a carefully hidden cage.

Within minutes, there were people all around him. He heard voices, but the cover that disguised the cave-cage remained and he could not see. He felt the cage being lifted and placed on a surface. Then a door slammed and a motor started. He recognized that he was in a car, and the scents of other dogs permeated his still quivering nostrils. A small urban rescue group had been informed of his frantic wanderings, and the volunteers had devised a way to capture the vagabond dog.

When the motor and movement stopped, Buffer again felt his cage being lifted, and then the welcome warmth of a new place seeped through the cover that blinded him. He was set down again and the cover was slowly lifted off his cage. Buffer blinked and his eyes watered as they became accustomed to the light of the room he was now in. Three women squatted down around him and spoke kindly. Although he had never heard such soft intonations, he felt a small tingle of curiosity creep into his mind.

One of the women gently opened the cage door so Buffer could come out, and although he had wanted nothing more just a short time earlier, he hesitated. He looked through the cage bars and saw that he was in a compact kitchen. It smelled like the food that had attracted him. There were also smells of other dogs and the scents of the people who were now focused on him. Through a slatted wooden gate at the inside doorway of the kitchen, small dog faces peered at him, and he heard their tiny noses sniffing. Buffer left the cage cautiously, scampered to the farthest corner of the room, and cowered under a chair.

Two of the women left. The one who remained placed a bowl of water and a bowl of food in the room, turned out the big lights, and lit a small light over the counter. She and the other dogs left Buffer, and he heard them in another part of the house. When all became quiet, he crept out of his corner, wolfed down the food, gulped the water, and carefully explored his new confinement area. He found a soft bed in a corner, and despite his attempt to stay alert and on guard, he fell into the deepest sleep he had experienced since his abandonment.

Over the next several weeks, Buffer was treated kindly by the lady who cared for him. She taught him tricks, and he played with the other little dogs who lived there. One by one, they left with new people and other small dogs came to stay. They were often as frightened as he had been, but he was soon able to entice them into games of chase around the house and tug-of-wars with squeak toys. Buffer was also included in walks outside on a leash.

Buffer's confidence grew. His growing trust in the lady enabled him to face new experiences, and he loved to learn skills that brought both praise and wonderful food treats. His ribs disappeared and his wide eyes held curiousity, not anxiety. When his lady introduced him to new people, he remained shy but was no longer afraid of being hurt.

When a nice older couple took him to their house, he regressed into his old fearfulness for a few hours, but they put no pressure on him. He quickly felt comfortable because these people also had wonderful treats and toys for him. They lived quietly and there was never any sound or sight that reawakened Buffer's panic from his lost days in the park.

Buffer remains in his adoptive home, and although he is still shy with strangers, he has not experienced the anxiety and panic he once knew. His life is filled with kindness, love, care, and warmth. He has been joined by another small rescue dog. The two of them have found courage in each other's presence and both trust their people.

LEARNING TO TRUST ONE PERSON

Trust is imperative to learning. No dog can learn when his brain is awash in stress hormones. Stress hormones cause "brain freeze." Brain freeze is the inability to function on any but the most primitive level of reaction. When a dog trusts, these hormones are tamped down by reasoning that has been learned through the experience, that there is one person who can be relied on for whatever resource he seeks, whether it is food or protection.

When a dog finds himself drowning in the hormones of fear, he can reach for the life preserver of trust he has in you, one person he has had positive interactions with. He can stay afloat above panic. He will learn to run to you, instead of away from you. When a relationship of trust buds between a timid dog and a caring person, the largest part of the battle towards socialization is over.

Trust is easier to attain when a fearful dog begins

with one person at a time. Dogs who routinely face a round-robin of caregivers (rescue or shelter staff) will initially learn that in general, people can be kind to them. But only when a relationship with one person is established can the fearful dog fully learn to trust people and accept life with humans. When a fearful dog is thrust into a panic situation and there is not a single person he trusts above all others, he may not be able to control himself. His reactions in the throes of panic could place him in danger.

For example, rescued puppy-mill dogs are known for their timid personalities. Throughout their lives they receive little socialization, medical care, or adequate nutrition. Their living conditions are substandard at best, and what contact they do have with humans is usually negative. When mill dogs are placed in foster or adoptive homes, they often become overwhelmed with the concentrated, well-intended attention their new people shower on them.

No longer ignored but intensely focused upon, these dogs panic. Fearful dogs are high escape risks. This is a common issue with dogs like mill rescues who have never been confined in close quarters with people, and with dogs whose only previous close experiences with people have been hurtful. When these confused dogs escape their new homes, they run fast and far away in directionless panic. If they are found, they rarely come to people they do not know, even if those people are trying to save them. But if there has been enough time for a dog to learn to trust one person, the bond between them may provide the lost dog with the courage to come to that person.

However, it is imperative that regardless of how bonded your fearful dog appears to be to you, he must *never be allowed off leash.* Primitive and long-lasting fear reactions may flood him at any time and in any scenario. A dog who is hardwired through breeding and who has been reinforced in his panic by poor treatment will remain a serious flight risk *forever.* Never take chances. Keep your dog leashed and in an escape-proof harness his entire life.

When his life is saved by rescue team efforts, it is essential that the fearful dog be allowed to bond with one person during his rehabilitation. Most dogs instinctively devote themselves to a family unit or so-called pack and seek a trustworthy leader. You can use that instinct to help your dog learn to trust your leadership. Later, you can help him transfer his attachment to other people if you plan to rehome him.

When you obtain an unsure dog, you must constantly monitor his comfort level with every aspect of his new life. Watch your dog for stress signals such as lip licking, yawning, averted eyes, cowering body, and (especially) attempts to get away from you. Be sensitive regarding your dog's ability to handle your direct eye contact, touch, and constant attention.

Often, at the beginning of time in your home, a shy dog may prefer some proximity to you but not focused attention by you. As you go about your daily life, keep noise at a minimum. Keep your body in softened postures, and your actions slow. Hum soft tunes so the dog always knows where you are. Sudden appearances around corners can throw a surprised dog into panic and set your relationship back in progress.

An unsure dog must be allowed to discover that physical closeness to you will always be a pleasant, comforting experience, not a source of instability and unpredictability. You must become his port in the storm of life: steady and true, trustworthy and stable. You must become his resource for all good things: food, water, companionship, play, and protection.

Read your dog's readiness to submit to touch, ability to be physically close, and increased relaxation in your company. With time, tolerance, and gentle treatment he will learn he can turn to you when he needs security.

Once a shy dog learns trust through positive outcomes with an initial person like you, he will more readily transfer that trust and cooperation to other people. This is especially true when a dog with a known abuse, neglect, or cruelty history consciously decides to give humans one more chance. Learning through connection, affection, and trust will result in quality lessons that will last the dog's lifetime.

Chapter 6

~<><>~

The Importance of Time

*T*he noose closed tight around the muscular Pit
Bull's neck. Her frantic struggle for freedom was
unsuccessful. Skittles gagged as she squealed in
panic. The men at the end of the noose pole reminded her
of the tormenter she had escaped from just days before.
Then one of the men encircled her ribs with his arms and
lifted her gyrating body. The brindle-colored dog was
thrown into the back of the animal control vehicle. They
released the noose and she could breathe again.

When the door banged shut, she had only slits in the
side through which to see light. The vehicle motor roared
to life, and Skittles felt herself hurtling through space.
Unique scents wafted into her dark chamber and she
pressed her nose against the stripes of light to catch any
hint of her fate.

When the vehicle finally came to a halt an hour later,
Skittles felt ill. She had never been in a vehicle before.
The door opened and the uniformed men slipped a leash

around her neck. A small tug from the man who held the other end of the leash caused Skittles to jump down on to the grass and sunlight of the shelter's front lawn. There she vomited. After she emptied what little was in her stomach, the men handed her over to other strange people. Skittles was turned loose in an indoor cinderblock kennel with a chain-link doorway. Alone and confined, she was afraid. She shuddered at the sound of other dogs' yips, howls, barks, and whines, and then she retreated to the farthest corner of her new prison.

Skittles was not yet one year old, but in her short life she had seen her mother taken away and had heard vicious dogfights. Gunpowder had been shoved up her nose in an attempt to cause pain and make her mean. She had been beaten by her breeders when she cowered in the wake of a snarling dog instead of fighting him. She had smelled death.

Instead of becoming aggressive, Skittles had become sensitive and fearful. The boundaries of her life were the inside of her wire cage and the fight ring inside the secretive dark building.

One morning when her fight trainer had again raised the stick he beat her with in his attempts to make her nasty, she dodged and was able to pull her rope leash out of his hand. She ran through fields she had never seen, under barbed-wire fences, over rock ledges, and through small streams of water, where she paused only long enough to lap a quick drink. Hours later, as she climbed out of a ravine, a shrub branch caught her rope noose. When she struggled to continue her flight, it pulled the noose off her neck.

Free to run unencumbered, Skittles continued her flight until she eventually tired and hid in an old raccoon den under a barn. Over the next few days, the rancher *noticed her pacing his property, searching and skinny. He put out food for her, and when she reliably showed up for it every morning, he called the county animal control officers. Her budding trust in the rancher's deliverance of food was shattered when the noose on the long stick tightened after they cornered her.*

Skittles' time in the shelter was to be short. She would not allow anyone to touch her, which made a behavior evaluation impossible. They scheduled her for euthanasia. The shelter personnel did not have time for the extensive behavior modification programs that a wild dog like Skittles would need to prepare her for adoption. She would never fit into the average household the way she was.

A woman who worked at the shelter often visited her in her kennel. Within a few days, Skittles allowed the woman to slip yet another noose leash over her head as the woman fed her treats. The woman led her outside. Frightened again, Skittles froze, which allowed the woman to lift her into her car. The woman drove Skittles to a house where she was met by another woman and three dogs. Then the woman who had brought her to the house left.

Skittles spent six months in her foster home. There she was allowed to run safely in the backyard, come and go through a dog door, sleep in the warmth of the house, and share a couch with the other dogs, who were nonthreatening and playful with each other and her. Skittles became attached to the big Lab mix. She watched skeptically when he solicited affection from the woman, but she followed him around the yard and copied every sniff and roll in the grass.

When all three dogs were leashed, each exhibited excited anticipation. Skittles just watched. Day after day she was left behind and alone. She understood that the leash was the key to going with her new dog family. Yet she remained too afraid to let the woman near.

Eventually, Skittles allowed a collar to be snapped on because her idol, the Lab, did. She stayed in the vicinity of the woman because he did, ate when he did, and slept fitfully while he snored next to her on the floor.

Skittles' foster caregiver evaluated all of Skittles' reactions and discovered the dog was fearless with everything in her environment except people. Skittles was afraid of hands, feet, legs, direct eye contact, moving arms, bending, and almost every normal human movement. It took six weeks before the woman could get out of a chair in the customary way without frightening Skittles. Instead, she had to consciously locate Skittles and turn away before she rose. If she entered the room Skittles chose as her safe place, Skittles jumped up, barked repeatedly, then ran out the dog door.

To earn the dog's trust, the woman fed Skittles delicious canned food from her hands, the tops of her feet, and on her knees. She held the food over Skittles' head, to her sides, and close to the ground. She never entered a room without humming songs, so Skittles could tell where she was and not be frightened by her sudden appearance into a room. She taught Skittles what the word "leash" meant and other basic obedience skills.

Skittles learned that the reward of a walk happened when she sat bravely for the woman to bend over her and attach a leash. She was finally included with the other dogs when they left the yard.

Although she remained timid, Skittles never displayed aggression, even when frightened, because her caregiver protected her from going "over threshold." She learned that although escape was always possible through the dog door, she actually needed it less and less. Finally, the only reason she used the door was to go outside to play or relieve herself. Her progress was slow but steady. Skittles was adopted six months after her capture by a couple who loved dogs like Skittles for exactly who they were.

Skittles continues to improve in her new home with her knowledgeable and patient owners and a "sister" dog—also brindle colored, and also very shy. She has taken car trips all over the country, played in the Pacific Ocean, swam in lakes, climbed mountains, and dug holes in beach sand.

Skittles needed time to trust her people and find a life of joy, safety, and emotional security. Her life was saved because people were willing to give her that time.

WHAT TIME CAN DO

Fearful dogs may be timid due to past treatment, genetics, lack of socialization, or like Skittles, a combination of all three. When you take on a fearful dog, your skill level, awareness, experience, patience, and leadership are important components of turning her around. But the most important component is time.

You will make mistakes. Some training techniques will not work and will have to be traded for others. You may discover new fears that the dog has and have to come up with ways to deal with them. Just when it seems you have made progress, the dog's development may reach a plateau, or backslide. The only real mistake you can make is to push. Rushing a fearful animal will fail, regardless of your experience and knowledge.

Time is the key to healing in a dog with fear issues. It is better to take too much time than not enough. The dog will tell you what she needs; you just have to learn how to listen. People want to know the history of a fearful pet so they can know how to *cure* the pet, but there is no cure. Fear can only be *managed*. History is not important; the here-and-now is. It does not matter why a dog is afraid, it does matter how you deal with it in her current life.

Although research has concluded that dogs do not have the cognitive ability to intellectually contemplate their future like people do, dogs are able to pull from a rich array of memories of past experiences. If a particular event, experience, or person resulted in over-threshold trauma, the dog will remember it. This is called a "fear memory."

A deeply ingrained fear memory will never be completely erased. Lesser fears will seem to be overcome but intense fears will continue to lurk deep inside the pet's primitive brain, the amygdala. The success of fear management depends on giving the dog time to recover and relearn.

When a fearful dog arrives in an adoptive or foster home, she needs time to become accustomed to that environment's routines with no pressure. No demands should be made other than to learn feeding and exercise times and other important requirements of living in the new home. Resident pets also need time free of demands to accustom themselves to the newcomer. Give them time and space to relate to each other and the newcomer in daily life. The newcomer will then find a reliable animal companion (usually of the same species, but not always) to mimic and learn from in her attempt to fit into the family pack dynamics.

Most fearful dogs will attach to another pet before they look to human leadership. When this attachment occurs, it becomes easier to make progress in socialization. Dogs have the ability to learn by observation, and a steady, reliable pet mentor can greatly aid your efforts.

Habituation becomes the first goal. A fearful new dog must become accustomed to the sights, sounds, smells, and physical characteristics of her new locale. As your fearful dog's leader, you should patiently, quietly, and confidently go about your routines. Be aware of the dog's mental processing of her new environment. Slow down and do whatever is necessary to help the dog see that there is no need for a fear reaction.

Some fearful dogs become anxious when they are the center of attention. You should conduct daily living activity without hovering, but keep an eye on the pet's attention and stress level. Indirect desensitization—the desensitization that occurs simply by ongoing exposure to common events in the environment—must be slowly and methodically approached with constant awareness of the dog's comfort. This is another advantage to foster homes. Shelters do not offer day-to-day informal living routines and activities that fearful dogs must be habituated to. Formal desensitization procedures will be necessary with specific fear producing stimuli, but the calmness of everyday living will keep the dog on an even keel emotionally.

When one-on-one attention to the fearful dog is necessary, as in structured desensitization and training, keep a low-key focus with averted eyes, softened body posture, and slow movements, which will lessen intensity in the interaction between you and the dog. If the dog exhibits stressed body language and/or behaviors, experiment with altering distance, the amount of time exposed, or the intensity of confrontation to fear producing stimuli. Make either written or mental notes of each day's progress.

If more than one person works with the dog, as in families, you should each keep written notes to inform each other of progress, techniques that work, and to avoid overexposure. Exposure to insecurity-producing stimuli should be short, frequent, and at a distance or intensity that is incrementally applied at slowly increasing levels to provide progress yet avoid overload or flooding.

When you and the dog become familiar with each other, your daily routines will become comfortable for her. At that point diversions from that routine can begin. These diversions will help her learn to accept fluctuations in her daily life. Rigidity in routine is ultimately not practical and is impossible over time, so once the dog has settled into a simple routine, slow variations can be developed to build flexibility in her ability to cope with novel experiences and stimuli.

Avoid setting goals that are too high. If you make mistakes in judgment, back up the exposure to the last successful level or even a bit farther if the error caused serious reactions in the dog. Her confidence and ability to perform to a positive reward level is the desired result. When errors occur, your steady attitude and calm demeanor can erase rising fear in the dog and head off knee-jerk limbic reactions.

There cannot be set schedules or predictable steps as a dog advances on her path to confidence. Many things impact a dog's progress. Inherent differences in breeds, sex, and genetic temperament result in varied abilities to process challenges. Missed crucial socialization periods in youth will set the dog behind in her social skills. The degree to which the dog has been subjected to cruelty, abuse, and neglect can result in deeply ingrained psychological preconditions. Medical issues can impair her physical and psychological adjustment to her new life.

Dedicate whatever time is necessary for the individual dog. It is not easy and it is not quick. It can be exhausting for you and her. But a relatively small investment of your time at the beginning will help the dog become behaviorally functional and socialized in her world. When she can smoothly integrate herself into a world of people and other dogs, her stress levels will lower, her behavioral reactions to novel stimuli will calm, and she will become a better adjusted dog psychologically. When your timid student has control of her fears, her quality of life will improve. She will no longer be at the mercy of her own uncontrollable reactions and her self-confidence will grow. With increased self-confidence, controlled behavior, and a happier temperament, your foster dog will become more adoptable. If she is your own dog, your relationship will deepen.

Whether you are preparing the dog for yourself or for others, the emotional closeness shared with a fearful dog who has conquered her demons, is different from any other in human life and can produce a depth of satisfaction, warmth, and peacefulness that no other partnership can. When your dog feels peace, she will trust you as her leader and she will continue to look to your for guidance when she needs it.

CHAPTER 7

─╱╲─

The Importance
of Leadership

*J*essie was born in an urban backyard. His family
pack was six Labrador-mix puppies and two
parents. All of the dogs lived in the garage and
yard, and the puppies were lovingly attended by their
parents. When the man of the house worked in the garage,
they wandered in and out. Otherwise their people treated
them kindly but without much interaction.

When Jessie was three years old, a severe winter
piled up snow against the backyard fence. Jessie and his
siblings learned that they could climb the pile and walk
over the top of the fence. They enjoyed running free around
their neighborhood and made the trip frequently during
the next several days. Their owner drove around in his
truck to find his dogs, loaded them in the open truck bed,
and took them home.

One morning Jessie and his siblings were loaded up
without escaping first. The man drove them to a shelter
where he relinquished them. The dogs were separated and

each was placed in an indoor kennel with cinderblock walls, concrete floor, and an eight-foot chain-link gate. Jessie could hear his dog family nearby but could not see them. While they awaited behavior and health evaluations, Jessie continually climbed his gate and dropped to the floor outside. He trotted down the aisle and paced in front of his brothers' gates. He stayed near them until shelter staff returned him to his own kennel.

Amiable yet shy, black-and-white Jessie was forever separated from his siblings when shelter staff placed him in an adoption kennel in the public area of the shelter the Wednesday after his relinquishment. Friday afternoon he was adopted by a young man and taken to an apartment. Jessie was well fed and walked on Saturday and Sunday. But on Monday morning he was confined to a crate. His young man worked and left Jessie alone all day.

Jessie had never been inside a house. He had never been alone or confined in a small box. He felt growing claustrophobia and was unable to cope with the new sensation of isolation. He panicked in the crate. It took him most of the day, but he managed to chew a hole through the hard plastic and escape into the apartment.

Immediately Jessie ran from door to window to another door. He could not find his way outside—the only comfortable environment he knew. Panting with anxiety, his bloody mouth left saliva stains throughout the apartment. In the process of looking for a way out, he shredded pillows, ripped open a couch, and yanked down blinds. He lost control of his bladder and bowels, which destroyed the carpeting.

When his owner returned from work, he yelled at Jessie. Noise sensitive and submissive, Jessie dropped into a heap on the floor. Within an hour Jessie was returned to the shelter.

Familiar people helped Jessie settle in for the next several days during which he was subjected to much attention from the training and behavior staffs. Thankful and appreciative for the activity and attention, Jessie tried to understand what they asked of him and happily bounced around them.

Four days after his return to the shelter, a new woman took Jessie's leash and led him out of the behavior office. She took him to a house where he lived as a foster dog for the next two months. He learned household manners and daily routines, and he had the companionship of the woman and her other pets, which included one old small dog, three cats, and two parakeets. Jessie calmed, put on weight, and responded quickly and intelligently to training.

People came and visited him. One Saturday, he left the house with a man and woman who took him for a car ride to the mountains. That night he found himself in another new home. The nice couple lavished attention on him. They spent all their time at home or on walks in the forest. There were scents of unfamiliar creatures everywhere. On one walk, Jessie found something delightfully stinky and ate it. That night his stomach churned.

His new owners had chosen that evening to leave him for the first time and go out to dinner, and they left before his first bout of nausea. He vomited again and again. When he had nothing left in his stomach, Jessie panicked at the quiet aloneness of his new home. Once again, he tried to find his way outside by attempting every escape route he could smell cold air through. Doors, windows, and anything in or around them were destroyed.

When the people returned, both yelled at him, which made his stomach-ache even worse. The house was a mess and the noxious odor of vomit and diarrhea was more than Jessie's people could bear. He was locked out of the bedroom, but he heard the loud voices of the couple arguing. Every now and then he heard his name, but he remained confused, sick, lonely, and insecure. He did not sleep, but lay pressed up against the closed bedroom door on the hard wood floor.

Jessie was returned to the shelter the next morning. A few hours later he was back in his foster home. Although happy to be reunited with his companions, Jessie vomited repeatedly. His foster caregiver once again returned him to the shelter. He was stuffed into a cage in the hospital and was too sick to fight confinement in the small metal area. Five days of medical treatments, medicines, and noise in the hospital left Jessie exhausted, skinny, and high-strung. On the sixth day, the woman who had fostered him returned and took him back to the house he had loved and the companions he had been comfortable with. He was adopted by his foster mistress. Jessie finally found a person willing to make a lifelong commitment to him, regardless of his anxieties.

One year later, under the tutelage of his final owner, Jessie passed behavior and training exams to become a humane education mascot for the shelter he came from. He loved the children he met in the shelter classrooms and on excursions to schools and churches. He visited senior centers and gently sat near folks in wheelchairs. Jessie became an excellently behaved ambassador for the shelter. They called him the quintessential shelter dog, and he was featured in fundraising events and television commercials.

The consistent, reliable leadership of Jessie's owner increased his self-confidence to the point where he is no longer afraid to be alone. Jessie often goes out his dog door and lays in his yard, watching birds and squirrels frolic around him. He sleeps on his own bed, in his own room, and seems to relish his privacy.

Because he no longer feels stress, his ability to learn has skyrocketed, and his owner brags that he is the smartest dog she has ever had. Jessie's faith in her guidance has transformed him from an anxious, high-strung, insecure dog to a pet with joy in each step, confidence in each challenge, and benevolent leadership towards every other foster dog who enters his home.

The Role of Leadership

Working with fearful dogs requires you to be a steady, trustworthy leader. This leadership role takes the pressure of the unknown off the dog, allowing him to feel less threatened by the unfamiliar world he has entered where people have power over life-sustaining resources such as food, water, shelter, safety, and companionship. Dogs are inherently social and look for leadership when it is physically and psychologically safe.

Dogs are social animals that are often referred to as pack animals. Canid packs (coyotes, wolves, and dogs) are raised by a family group and have organized social structures within those families. Every pack family has a hierarchy with leaders and followers. Pack membership and hierarchy place are crucial elements to psychological security in a dog.

Insecure dogs have an even greater need for kind but definite leadership. They can become pathologically needy when the person who provides safety through structure is absent or ceases to act as leader. For instance, when an owner becomes ill or absent, their dog may experience anxiety, which may be manifested by out-of-character behaviors—a sure symptom of something amiss in the dog's emotional life. These dogs are the most prone to anxiety-produced destructive behaviors. But, as in Jessie's case, increased confidence built through trust in a strong leader can support the development of the dog's true personality, and his clingy behavior often decreases.

In domestic dogs, a family group hierarchy is fluid. For example, Jessie became the yard guard, but his owner's other dog was the one who barked at visitors at the front door inside. The second dog followed Jessie's lead when they were in the yard, but when they were in the house, Jessie followed his companion's lead. When both were unsure, they looked to their owner for guidance and security. Dogs can transfer their need for leadership from each other to people, but if their people are inadequate leaders, household dogs will establish a hierarchy of their own, which may lead to challenging behavioral problems.

Dogs in a household pack choose which of their members will take the role of leadership in various situations. Their owners must allow to them to do so, except in situations where the owner's leadership is crucial. For example, if both Jessie and his companion bark at the door, their owner must be able to control them to allow visitors to come in safely and without chaos. The dogs must learn to trust the owner to protect them and their home property. Only with trust in the owner's leadership can the dogs accept what they consider to be intruders. Such dogs rarely become nuisance barkers or fence fighters. Dogs who have trust in their leader will also tolerate new experiences, people, and things.

CANINE BEHAVIOR AND LEADERSHIP

Wildlife research biologist L. David Mech's landmark studies of wolves determined that wolf packs in the wild (as opposed to forced non-family packs in captivity) do not have dominant and submissive hierarchies as humans had defined them. He postulated that wolf packs were families in which the parents were leaders of the pups, even when they were full grown. Pups of different generations often stayed within the group when new litters arrived, but none of the younger wolves challenged the parents for leadership.

Temple Grandin, the famous animal behaviorist, suggests in her book *Animals Make Us Human* that pet dogs do not need to be *dominated* by their pseudo-pack leaders, humans. Instead, she feels that dogs need replacement mothers and fathers to *guide* them through their lives with their human families.

Through specialized breeding we have neotenized (kept in an immature state) our companion dogs. Because dogs never completely mature emotionally, they are in constant need of parental guidance, especially in the world they inhabit with people. Dogs that live in dense human populations, such as cities, need to be taught socially acceptable behaviors. Once taught, they are like children, in the sense that they maintain their learning more successfully with continued encouragement and praise for proper performances. The old techniques of dog training relied on dominance/submission theories, such as "showing him who is boss," "how to establish yourself as pack leader," etc. These philosophies often lead to cruelty, abuse, and heavy-handed disciplinary tactics that only frighten, confuse, and hurt dogs. Modern research has repeatedly shown that positively reinforcing proper behaviors, while ignoring negative ones, is far more successful in helping dogs understand what we expect from them. Reward-based interactions have been more successful at increasing communication, controlling behavior reliably, and lessening fear in dogs. The bullying tactics of establishing human dominance over pet dogs has backfired in numerous ways, but none as spectacularly as when interacting with an insecure and shy dog.

A fearful dog needs the guidance of a confident leader who will help him find his place in his family pack and the human society he is part of. Like children, dogs need to know how to behave in a domestic social setting. Limits, rules, and patient teaching of household manners are required by the human parent to teach the dog how to obtain rewards and encouragement. Without manners, the dog, like the child, will have no idea how to behave.

When a child or a pet is disciplined for something he did wrong without being taught what the appropriate behavior is, he becomes confused and afraid of authoritative leadership. But when taught what the social rules are, he will accept the leader and have more confidence in his own behavior. The dog will also be welcomed in the wider human-dominated society his family is a part of.

FEAR DOMINANCE VS. LEADERSHIP

The leader who inspires fear is a bad leader. Hundreds of world citizens who live under political, religious, and social dictatorships can attest to the frustration and resentment that builds when there are inhumane, unequal rules in that society. If rules are inconsistent, not applicable to the powerful, or are randomly exhibited displays of dominance by the leader, unrest will result.

Children who receive no consistent instruction on acceptable behavior in their society will become adults who have no idea how to conform or contribute to that society. If treated cruelly because they do not fit in, children evolve into rebellious individuals who are confused and resentful. Growing anger will develop into violence, and so the cycle will repeat itself, when the frustrated child becomes a parent.

Dogs will act out just as citizens poorly governed and children poorly taught will. Dogs must be taught how to fit into human society. Socially unacceptable dog behavior is often cruelly and insensitively crushed by owners, which only intensifies fear in dogs who are already anxious and creates fear in a pet who has not previously been insecure.

When frustrated dogs grow up, various forms of aggression can result, and most is fear-based. Fear aggression behavior in dogs can almost always be tied to confusion; very little aggression is genetic. Human behavior is complex, even to other humans. As intuitive and aware as most dogs are in their attempts to understand people (by dog cognitive standards), they often end up more confused. Lack of consistency in human behavior is the most common and the most confusing for dogs. Confusion sprouts into fear.

Unpredictability in human behavior is unsettling to any dog. Human behavior is rife with nuance, subliminal messages, and ulterior motives, all of which are impossible for dogs to unravel. When their human leader behaves in ways that a dog cannot interpret, fear is often the result. The ignorant owner often punishes his dog when the dog is only confused, not deliberately disobeying. Dog behaviors based on the dog's desire to avoid punishment are often misinterpreted by his people.

DO DOGS REBEL AGAINST LEADERSHIP?

Dogs are primarily nonverbal in their own pack societies and communicate with each other through body language. Dogs are visual and watch human body movements with fluency. Humans are not aware of our unpredictable and conflicting messages to our dogs because we have lost the conscious art of reading body language. We depend on verbal communication. When our body contradicts our verbal commands, a dog will trust what she reads in our movements over what we say. When a dog responds to what she reads in our posture and movements, she can be mistakenly accused of ignoring or rebelling against our verbal commands.

A common example of this miscommunication is when a person calls out "Come" to a dog. The person walks forward to greet the dog, bends over the dog, reaches out, smiles, and makes direct eye contact. Bending straight forward is intimidating to dogs. Reaching towards the dog may invade her personal space and smiling is baring teeth. Direct staring and squinting while smiling are other signs of aggression. Straight-on approach is also intimidating, especially if it is fast. No peaceful dog-to-dog interaction will include these postures.

Unless a dog is highly socialized and fluent in the language of "human," the last thing she will do is come if these body postures are evident. The caller may interpret the dog's avoidance as disobedience and find fault with the dog. People rarely associate their body language with the dog's reticent behavior.

Dogs respond to clarity in communication and clarity for them is the closest approximation of their own language, which is nonverbal body language. Dogs rarely ignore human verbal commands. They either do not understand the request or see human body language as a clearer message. Without repetitive reward-based training, dogs may not know the proper response to the request. Seeking approval, an unsure dog will try to figure out what to do. Often, a confused dog will run through the performance of known behaviors in an attempt to discover which one will appease her person, elicit a reward, or return peaceful coexistence between the person and herself. People often see this run-through of repertoires as rebelling against or *ignoring* the given command, not *ignorance* of the command. Unfortunately, misinterpretation of a dog's behavior results in punishment for the dog, not understanding in their person.

PUNISHMENT

In her book *Mother Knows Best* puppy trainer Carol Lea Benjamin points out that a mother dog does not yell, hit, or physically hurt her puppies when she trains them in proper dog etiquette during the crucial first eight weeks with her and their litter mates. Few puppies are afraid of their mother. They trust her because she never goes beyond the intensity of correction needed to obtain puppy obedience. She makes it known what she expects, praises affectionately, and disciplines in ways they understand. No dog punishes another.

Physical punishment by people is the result of lack of emotional control in the person who holds power. For some people there is a perverse pleasure in administering physical or psychological pain to subordinates such as children or dogs. But punishment does not teach anything but fear. Responses based in coercion will disappear when the dominant person cannot wield power. That is why so many dogs trained with the old school compulsive techniques of physical domination "disobey" when the threat is absent. They do not learn to perform a request out of desire to obtain reward.

Nowadays, physical punishment for children is frowned upon and many studies have proven its inability to constructively produce responsible, confident children that fit into human society. But people still think punishment works with pet dogs. Instead, the compassionate parent and pet trainer uses humane correction to guide their child or their dog to desirable behavior.

CORRECTION

Correction is not punishment. Correction stops an inappropriate behavior and teaches an appropriate one. Knowing the difference between correction and punishment is important. Humane correction and redirection are good leadership tools. They are invaluable tools when teaching the fearful dog.

If a dog indulges in undesirable behavior, a good leader will ignore it and redirect the dog with positive reward for a desirable action. Undesirable behavior should be ignored to avoid inadvertent reinforcement. Because dogs are dependent on social interaction, behavior that does not result in attention will be abandoned. Ignored behavior will eventually become extinguished. However, shortly before an undesirable behavior dies out an "extinction burst" will occur. This is when the dog attempts to obtain your attention by frequent and intense performance of the undesirable behavior.

Ignoring an extinction burst is easier said than done. Some dogs, like stubborn children, can become amazingly annoying in their intensity. Dogs, like children, learn quickly how to break down a weakened parent/trainer. You must continue to ignore the behavior repertoire, for the dog will see even the slightest reaction (positive or negative) as reinforcement, and she will continue the behavior.

If the dog's behavior must be stopped immediately, as in dangerous scenarios, redirect the dog away from the problem activity with an immediate distraction. Then guide the dog to a rewardable behavior. Guidance to a rewardable behavior will help the dog learn success and gain confidence because she has found a behavior that reengages her with you. Reengaging a fearful dog is a real accomplishment, and proves her growing trust and eagerness to learn.

RECONNECTION WITH THE LEADER

Once the unwelcome behavior has ceased, a trusting dog will look to her leader for a way to emotionally reconnect. At that point you can redirect the dog into a positive behavior and reward. Often just interaction is enough reward for a highly social dog and works especially well with fearful dogs. Punishment will drive a fearful dog away from reconnection and permanently harm your relationship.

Dogs do not tolerate emotional or physical separation from others well. Often, the only correction a dog needs is to have you cease interaction by standing quietly. For major infractions, turning away and standing still will reboot the dog's attention and desire to learn and reconnect. The benevolent dog leader always immediately forgives, forgets, and guides the dog to appropriate interaction through verbal and physical praise, play, and time together.

Fearful dogs are more susceptible to permanent emotional damage and are in special need of benevolent behavioral correction, emotional connection, cognitive redirection, heartfelt praise, and physical contact. Use whatever reward she finds most valuable. When a fearful dog is settled into her routine, confident in you, and showing less stressful behaviors, socialization groundwork has been laid. Structured training can begin. Skills taught through basic obedience training will further bond the dog to you, but will also provide attributes that will help her fit into human society. Fitting in is especially important if the dog is to be placed for adoption.

Business management school studies have shown that the best leaders are humble. Unpretentious leaders listen and learn from their subordinates. They are also subtle in their leadership, guiding by example and encouragement. The most successful leaders never succumb to dominant manipulation or subversive cruelty. Humble human leaders can make effective dog leaders as well, especially for insecure dogs.

How can you apply business management skills to dog training? By remaining humble and not arrogant, you can instinctively allow your pet to be herself around you. The dog is constantly alert to your reactions towards her and she is sensitive about whether she is engaging in behaviors that you will reward or chastise. Timid dogs are easily intimidated, and like easily intimidated employees, they will be hesitant in their responses, especially if they are afraid of making mistakes.

Fearful dogs are not only afraid of things, people, and situations, they are afraid to make decisions about their own behavior.

A large part of training and relationship building with a dog is similar to managing people: you must give your dog the opportunity to think. Constant dictating of behavior forces an insecure dog into submission, not independent thought. It is the same as micromanaging an employee. No one enjoys having someone look over their shoulder, pass judgment, and criticize. Shy dogs need encouragement and opportunities to be creative in their responses.

Learn to watch and listen to your insecure dog. She will tell you how she is receiving the information you are imparting. Be aware of the speed of her comprehension. Respect her abilities and be compassionate if she has trouble understanding. Never punish. Instead, guide with positive rewards and praise, and only correct when you are sure she understands but chooses her own path. Even then, remain open to the possibility that her own path in behavior is the best pathway for her, as an individual animal.

Your behavior must be trustworthy, allowing her to have confidence that you will teach her in benevolent ways. She must have confidence that when she behaves in ways she has been trained to believe are appropriate, she will gain your approval. When you treat your dog with compassion, respect, and patience, she will trust herself to make correct behavioral decisions.

CHAPTER 8

—╱╲—

Learning Theory

O nce trust is established between you and your fearful dog, and she looks to you for leadership in her learning, you may begin structured obedience training. Structured training requires formal sessions of one-on-one time with your dog. Goals should be defined by task and progression tracked. Each session should build to progress from the previous one, adding building blocks of physical and verbal vocabulary and skills, from simple to more challenging.

Unless the dog has physical limitations due to injury, genetics, or cognitive impairments such as dementia, basic obedience skills can be taught at any age. It is important for you to understand how dogs learn so we will discuss what are commonly referred to as the "ABCs of learning theory," and we will customize these steps to our fearful dog's rehabilitation. Let's review what we should know about training techniques for the fearful dog.

THE ABCs OF LEARNING THEORY AND REHABILITATION

Darwin labeled social animals like dogs "large brained" because their frontal lobes comprise a larger percentage of their overall brain structure than less social or "smaller brained" species, such as reptiles and amphibians. The frontal lobes hold the higher functions such as the ability to make decisions, understanding the consequences of actions, and control of emotions. These inherent abilities can be used when you teach a dog to control his fear reactions and focus on learning.

The key to success in teaching or training social animals like dogs is to discover what motivates them to want to learn. In other words, what does the dog value and how can those items of value be used to motivate? Is the dog food motivated? If not, will his favorite toy motivate him to pay attention? Motivators might include food, verbal and/or physical praise, toys, or anything that the dog finds valuable and desirable.

Primary motivators are tools (such as food treats) used in the beginning to help teach the dog the connection between the request for a behavior and the performance of that behavior. Later, when he knows the behavior well and automatically performs it when requested, the primary motivator can be replaced with a secondary motivator (such as verbal praise or physical affection). When you discover what motivates your dog, the application of learning theory in training becomes possible and successful.

Learning theory is the basis of understanding how brains acquire, store, and apply new knowledge. The

three steps to learning—the ABCs of learning theory—
are the antecedent, the behavior, and the consequence.

An antecedent (the "A" in the ABCs) is the presentation
of a request for a behavior. For example, one way to teach
your dog to sit is to request the action by vocal command
and/or hand signal. Because the uneducated dog has
no idea what the word or hand signal means at first, a
motivator such as a food treat can be used to help "bait"
the dog into the posture. You might move the treat over
his head with the future hand signal position (a hand held
flat, turned up, with the treat in between your fingers). As
the dog's head looks up to the treat, his hindquarters will
drop. When his hocks hit the ground in the sit position,
you immediately release the food into his mouth. With
time and repetition, the dog comprehends that the word,
the hand, and the treat come together when he puts his
rear end down and leaves his front end up (the sit posture).
The hand plus the treat will eventually teach the dog to
associate the formal hand signal (raising your flattened
hand from your thigh to your waist with your elbow bent
next to your waist) with the nonverbal command.

The "B" in the ABCs is the performance of the
requested behavior. Simple one-syllable/one-word
requests can eventually expand to more words with more
syllables and eventually a few words can ask for multiple
behaviors. Advanced training can yield long chains of
behavior as used in competitions (of obedience, agility, or
herding, for instance) and disability assistance. They are
also used in law enforcement with "sniffer" dogs.

Consequence is the "C" in the ABCs of learning theory.
Desired and undesired behaviors have consequences.
The dog who sits on command, as described above,

receives a tasty treat. The consequence can also be called the "reward," but not all consequences are rewards. If you request a behavior and the dog does not perform it (provided the dog knows what is expected), the consequence may be that no treat is given. This is a negative consequence, or withholding of reward. Dogs are naturally social, so when rewards are withheld, most dogs will look for new ways to obtain the reward and the attention that goes with it. That is when you re-request and redirect the dog to the appropriate behavior so he can earn his reward.

Withdrawal of contact with his leader is often the only motivation the dog needs to be led to desired behavior. Mild disapproval by withdrawing attention is enough to make most dogs search for ways to reconnect with you. This is a perfect opportunity to redirect undesirable behavior into rewardable action and renewed attention. Teaching desirable behavior and discouraging negative behavior by offering or withdrawing rewards is called "positive reinforcement" training.

Reinforcement will encourage a behavior to continue. Positive reinforcement is the arrival of good consequences—food, play, praise. Negative reinforcement is the removal of a bad consequence—for example, the elimination of the high-pitched squeal of an anti-barking device when a vocalizing dog quiets.

Types of punishment can also be considered positive or negative but punishment does not work humanely, especially with fearful dogs. Because of that, I will not discuss punishment details in this book.

Basic knowledge of learning theory is necessary when you teach fearful dogs, whether you are a professional trainer, a foster caregiver, or an owner. Being able to spout

out the technical terms is not important; understanding the concepts and how to use them is.

Understanding how to motivate a fearful dog in a positive way is valuable because they, of all dogs, are supersensitive to harshness, punishment, isolation, and corrections, especially if they do not understand what is expected of them. Anxious dogs must have the time to allow initial reaction stress hormones to settle before they can absorb new learning. They need more time to comprehend lessons and find self-confidence through rewardable performance. Fearful dogs cannot be punished or they will revert back to knee-jerk fear reactions, which will slow or halt further progress in learning.

As a rehabilitator you must be prepared to provide constant monitoring of the dog's reactions, calm approaches in presenting new material, and consistency in your reinforcements.

HABITUATION AND CURIOSITY

One aspect of fear that is ironic and little known is that fear sometimes stimulates curiosity. In *Animals in Translation*, Temple Grandin noted that fearful animals are often curious. Curious dogs may place themselves in danger, even those with timid personalities.

One dangerous example is the curiosity dogs exhibit around snakes. The sound and movement of rattlesnakes especially catch their attention. It is the sound of the rattle and the wiggle of the tail tip that draws dogs close. They have no way to know that the snake, who appears to be inanimate and is holding still in a coil, can lash out in a split second and bite. Dogs have no cognitive ability to associate a bite to the poisonous consequences of their curiosity. They certainly cannot predict the consequences of snake venom. All mammals have some innate fear of snakes, but not all heed the fear. If the dog has encountered other snakes with no consequence, he has habituated to them and has no reason to avoid investigation of another one—perhaps the dangerous rattler. This is an example of when you must monitor your dog's fear *and* his curiosity.

DESENSITIZING FEARFUL DOGS

Desensitization is gradually increasing intensity of a fear stimulus, so the dog can accept what frightened him. For example, if a dog is frightened of thunder, the sound of thunder can be recorded and played at whatever volume and distance from the dog that does not trigger a reaction.

Over time, either slowly increase the volume or slowly decrease the distance. Do not attempt to do both at once. They cannot be modulated at the same time. When the dog is desensitized to the sound or the distance, the opposite fear stimulus can be increased. If the dog reacts, the progression of exposure was too quick. Desensitization programs take a long time and cannot be rushed. (Note: The dog may be reactive to the static in the air prior to a thunderstorm, in which case the program will have to include that fear stimulus as well as the sound.)

Intensity (density, number, movement speed), distance (proximity, height, depth), variety (types of stimuli—olfactory, kinesthetic, visual, auditory, or gustatory), and volume (sound, pitch) cannot be increased at the same time. Only one stimulus at a time may be exposed for desensitization and habituation. When the dog is comfortable with one fear stimulus, gradual exposure to another may begin.

By using the ABCs of Learning Theory, you will be able to communicate with your fearful dog, and he will gain assurance in his ability to understand and please you. His eagerness to learn will increase, and his anxiety will decrease. As your relationship of trust evolves, your dog student will become more dependent on you for guidance and leadership. You will have become his protector, teacher, parent, and best friend. He no longer lacks what other fearful dogs do—self-confidence found from having a reliable advocate.

CHAPTER 9

--/|\--

Self-Confidence
and Advocacy

Fearful dogs lack two crucial and primary life resources: self-confidence and appropriate advocacy. Without self-confidence your timid dog will not seek out learning. If she does not find learning pleasant and dreads facing criticism, she will not reach out for your guidance. She will remain in a cocoon of insecurity, cower in exposure to novel stimuli, and never feel at peace in her own skin—much less in the human world she inhabits.

When your dog gains confidence in your steady support, she will know you can be counted on to intervene when she does not know how to deal with a situation or thing. Then her self-confidence will grow. Even the most fearful dog will investigate new challenges, if she knows her person is at her side with encouragement.

Self-Confidence

There are five reasons dogs do not possess the confidence to face things that frighten them. 1) They do not have experience with exposure to new environments. 2) They are not socialized to new people or other animals. 3) Varied past experiences have taught them to be insecure. 4) Genetic hardwiring of temperament has rendered them overly sensitive and reactive. 5) They have a mixture of 1–4.

Like people, the more success a dog has in dealing with real-life scenarios, the more she will trust her own judgment. Intelligent, social animals like dogs are capable of calm reasoning. Once your dog is exposed to a variety of nonthreatening experiences and objects and taught that she has control over her own involvement, her confidence in determining a course of response will grow. She will become more independent in her decision making and less timid in her choices as time progresses.

Dogs have prodigious memories and possess underappreciated reasoning abilities. Fearful dogs can be taught coping skills to self-calm and cognitively determine the need for a reaction, whether the reaction is to fight, flee, or ignore. This learned ability to reason in a controlled way empowers the dog's psyche and builds her confidence, which lessons her anxiety and insecurity.

Fearful dogs can be taught through household routine that anxiety is unnecessary. Most dogs live with people in protected environments, so they face less immediate danger to their survival than other animals. With exposure to previous fear stimuli through daily routine, they can habituate to each and learn to choose less reactive responses than running, barking, or fear-based aggression.

Because dogs have a long domestic history with people, they are usually quick to trust the leadership of a human and look to that person for reaction. If a dog has no peaceful or kind treatment history with people, it may take her more time to trust your leadership. But she will observe you, even if she does not appear to be.

If you do not respond with fear, the dog may calm herself. When she accomplishes this feat, she will lose more of her anxiety and gain self-confidence. Every anxious dog you work with needs your assistance in her development of confidence in novel situations and environments. Even if stimuli are similar to past exposures, she must be helped to generalize her processing of how to deal with each situation or item. She may become habituated to a fear producing stimuli in one environment but be taken aback in a new environment. Methodical, controlled reexposure and your support will make her fluent in every scenario, and she will transfer cognitive logic from one situation to another.

When a dog is able to make rational decisions pertaining to possible danger, she is engaging the secondary emotional brain of the cerebral cortex, not the primitive amygdala or limbic brain of nonrational panic. This allows her to realistically evaluate the situation and determine a course of action, based on dog logic. Once stress hormones dissipate—or are never secreted— reasoning will dominate and the dog's self-confidence increases.

SUPPORTING THE TIMID DOG

Once an insecure dog enters your world, she needs time to learn what you expect. Early in her cohabitation with you, while she learns and adjusts, she will need your emotional and physical support. She will need you to protect her from unknown and unforeseen events that may compromise her confidence, or even her life.

You will become your dog's protector and her resource for all good things. Examples of "good things" are food, water, shelter, and medical care. In the eyes of a dog, good things include play, treats, toys, prime resting places, proximity to you, exercise, and interaction with other dogs. It is important to understand that for the sake of the dog, good things also include guidance, patience, and removal of fear stimuli.

People who live with fearful dogs must be aware of keys that predict anxiety and learn to spot possible fear stimuli, or triggers, before there is time for the dog to react. The main key is to stay one step ahead of her—to see before she sees, to hear before she hears, to feel before she feels—in order to see the world through her eyes before she has time to react in limbic panic.

Environmental control (removing possible fear stimuli, timely desensitization, gentle habituation, and consistent positive reward-based treatment) will curb reactions before fear has a chance to erupt. When prediction is not possible or you make a mistake and miss an opportunity to block a negative experience, you should remain calm and nonreactive. This will allow the dog to observe and imitate you.

Although apes learn how to imitate complex behaviors from other members of their troop, such as fashioning tools, dogs seem limited in their ability to learn by observation. However, because you are her leader, your dog will look to you for your response to, what seems to her, a frightening stimulus. If she does not see a stressful reaction in you, she will be able to use the other skills you have taught her for self-comforting. She may jump into a safe place, return to your side, or retreat behind you.

Unsure dogs also seek out other dogs to learn appropriate reactions from. Fostered or new resident dogs will look to older resident dogs for their reactions and can learn from calmer, more socialized companions. Care must be taken to prevent fearful dogs in rehabilitation from being housed exclusively with other fearful dogs. If they are, whoever is worse will hold back learning progression for all. The exception is when one dog's fear triggers are different than another's. Sometimes two dogs whose fears are different can trade courage—when one is frightened, the other is not. In this case, the two dogs can help each other with their respective issues.

PROTECTING YOUR PET

Yet there may be times when it will be necessary to intervene in dog-to-dog interactions in order to protect your own pet. Not all dogs are receptive and one of the most common forms of dog aggression is that of dog-to-dog. When you and your dog come in contact with ignorant owners and their dogs, you must watch dog body language carefully. Most people are focused on other people (you) and ignore the dogs around them. Keep a close eye on the nonverbal conversation occurring between your dog and any others. Do not hesitate to pull your dog away from an escalating conflict and move on.

On occasion, you may also be required to protect your fearful dog from other hazards. Dogs allowed off-leash when they are not one hundred percent verbally controlled may run into the path of cars, be attacked by coyotes, or bitten by hidden snakes. Protection involves commonsense physical restraint for your dog's own good.

Appropriate Advocacy

One of my foster dogs was an extremely fearful medium-sized mixed breed dog named Snuggles. I found that physical exercise helped Snuggles control her anxiety. One day, we walked in a nearby park. I did not know Snuggles well and was still in the behavior evaluation process. Snuggles was a formerly lost dog of unknown history, so we passed the children's play area by circling in a wide arc around it. Closeness to noisy, active children is not advisable for fearful dogs, and my goal that day was only exercise, not habituation. Several children left the swing set and ran towards us. They screamed and waved their arms in their excitement.

The dog froze in fear. Then, in a split-second, Snuggles stiffened her body, barked a cacophony of vicious barks, and lunged forward on the leash. I had never seen a blatant fear-aggressive reaction in her before and knew that if I let go of the leash, I would not be able to catch her again because she was afraid of people and would never go to strangers.

I pulled her back, stepped in front of her, and told the children to stop. They continued to run towards us, every little body in incongruent activity, high-pitched noise, and motion. I escalated my voice volume and lowered my tone in firmness. Three of the children stopped and looked at me, with budding consternation on their faces. I had a moment of sadness. I did not want the children to be afraid of me. But that emotion was fleeting because I realized that the dog behind me was in a state of limbic panic and was my first object of loyalty and concern.

The smallest boy, barely five years old, continued to run to us. There were no parents in sight. I stepped forward and made myself as large as I could. I squared my shoulders, spread my legs, bent forward, and yelled in a deep and serious tone, "Stop! Now!" All the while, my foster dog continued barking, although she stayed behind my firmly planted legs.

Still the boy ran to us, oblivious to my commands, body language, and tone. He was in a craze of enthusiasm. When he reached me, I bent farther forward, placed my spread hand on top of his head, and physically stopped his forward movement. Only then did he seem to come out of his frenzy. His drive to maniacally run suddenly quieted. After a second of shock, he burst into tears.

At first, I felt furious and alarmed, and I wondered where the responsible parents were. I also realized what could easily have befallen my dog at the hands of the courts if she had been able to harm this boy, regardless of the situation. I was overcome with mixed emotions. I knew I had to instantly calm myself for Snuggles' sake, but also so I could provide a no-holds-barred education to these unattended children about safety around dogs they did not know.

I had given hundreds of classes on how to meet a dog as a professional humane educator for a large city shelter, but I had always taught in the sterility of a classroom environment I controlled, where my emotions were neutral and easygoing. This situation was different. My foster dog was in danger. If I had been unable to control the children, they could have been in danger from the dog. Snuggles had every right to protect herself, yet I knew that if small children were bitten, she would pay the price with *her life. And because she was not my dog—the shelter owned her—the morass of legalities could have become a nightmare. At the least, it would have culminated in my dismissal from the volunteer work of rehabilitating fearful dogs, work I deeply loved.*

How often does a dog owner allow their dog's personal space be violated by people or other dogs? When their dog is jumped on, dominated, or frightened by another dog, why does the owner apologize when their dog reacts with fear or aggression towards the interloper? Why accept the excuse from the other owner that their dog is just being friendly?

We are our dogs' advocates. We must protect them, especially when we know what our dog likes and dislikes in contact with others, whether animal or human. Never apologize for your dog when she tells you or an intruder what she needs, wants, or does not like. Protecting her psyche is as important as protecting her body.

Listen to your dog. She trusts you to know what she says and places her confidence in you to act on her behalf. If you react with inaction, ignorance, or your own embarrassment/or submission through apologies to the other person, you will betray her trust. Once her trust in you is eroded, it will be difficult to rebuild her confidence in your guardianship when she is frightened. Do not allow your own insecurities about how other people think of you make you fail in your advocacy. Your first loyalty must be to your dog. It may be a life-or-death devotion.

CHAPTER 10

━╸╱╿╲╺

Habituating a Fearful
Dog to People

D ogs who have learned to be afraid of people often
have good reasons for their fear. When we begin
rehabilitating a dog who has specific learned
fear memories of people, our work is harder than helping
the dog accept things like open umbrellas, big purses,
or flowing coats. If a dog trusts people but is afraid of
things, she will be more willing to approach the feared
object with her human protector at her side.

However, if a dog is afraid of people, you will have
a difficult job in rehabilitation. Distrust of people is a
unique obstacle to overcome. Overcoming fear to a thing
requires proximity to that thing. If a dog is afraid of
people, a nearby person will present a complex dilemma.
Rehabilitation work requires that the dog and person be
physically close to each other. It is necessary to touch
the dog. The dog must accept human movement. The
dog's survival (acceptance into and ability to remain in a
new home) requires that she be a physical, as well as an

emotional, companion to people. Without these criteria, a homeless dog is not considered adoptable.

Consequently, rehabilitation of specific human-based fear in dogs is the most important, and often the most difficult, work to be successful at in the wide spectrum of possible stimuli that cause fear. Starting off on the right foot is crucial. The ability to be physically close to a dog who is afraid of people will make or break the dog's future.

APPROACH

Initial approaches to a fearful dog can be frightening for the animal and dangerous for you. Learning safe handling skills is important, and respecting a dog's personal space avoids triggering a boundary violation in her. Imposing oneself on another is rude, regardless of the species. Unless the dog is injured and needs immediate medical treatment, respectful approach should consist of relaxed posture, indirect eye contact, sideways bending or getting on the ground at the dog's level. Constant awareness of your own safety must govern positioning, but the goal is to appear less intimidating.

If a dog has never been handled or has very limited experience with gentle human handling, it may take time for her to allow touch. In the early stages of socialization, you should not make demands on the inexperienced pet. Begin by being nearby. Do not ask for interaction. Sit or stand at the dog's height level if it is possible and safe to do so. Let her approach you when she is comfortable. Remember, fearful animals are often curious. It may take time for some dogs to feel able to approach. If the dog is in your home, several quiet sessions a day will speed her ability to be around you. If the dog is in a facility, try to manage as many sessions alone with her as possible in a day. Habituation takes time and frequency of low-intensity contact.

When the dog approaches or shows enough comfort to move around in your presence, gently and slowly throw a food treat somewhere in the vicinity of the animal but not *at* her. If she startles, she will look in your direction and when her full attention is on you, throw another treat. Avoid fast, jerky throws. Use slow underhanded tosses that gradually shorten the distance between you and the food. Dogs may become anorexic under duress, so do not be surprised if she is not food motivated.

A toy may be a higher value enticement, but avoid throwing it with an overhead arm movements. Do not bounce balls hard and high. Rolling balls on the floor may elicit her hesitant "prey drive" move to intercept it, which you should follow with gentle encouraging verbal praise. A supply of balls may gradually draw her closer as she picks up on the fact that you will provide another rolling "victim" in her hunt game. Prey drive can also be engaged with a stuffed toy or squeak toy. If the dog appears to be noise sensitive, abandon the squeaky and avoid training clickers.

Be aware of the dog's response to any noise a toy can make, because dogs who have never had toys may be frightened of novel sounds, especially if they come from your hands. Her association with your hands should only be positive. However, some dogs are instantly attracted to the sound of a "hunting victim," which is what a squeak toy is meant to mimic. Terrier breeds are especially prone to be engaged with squeaks. Allow the dog to investigate the toy, then slowly pick it up and squeeze it gently for a quiet squeak. Watch the dog's reaction. If the dog shies away and appears to be afraid, discontinue use of the squeaker. If the dog shows timid to intense interest, try to engage the dog in gentle play. This would be an excellent start for rapport, for play is a bonding experience in the dog world. Unsocialized dogs have probably never played with a person.

Never take a toy away from a dog who is afraid of you. Have many toys available in case the dog engages long enough to run off with the first toy. Do be in a confined area where the dog cannot run far, though. Throw a second or a third toy, then entice the dog to come closer to you for the fourth. If it becomes necessary to gather the toys, offer food treats in trade.

Dogs, especially fearful dogs, should never feel you are taking resources *from* them, only that you are the source of *giving* those valued resources. Wait to clear the space of toys until the dog has left the area, so she does not cognitively connect you to the disappearance of the things she shows interest in. Most dogs quickly learn that people give and people take—that people have power. Fearful dogs are sensitive to those they see having power over them, so attempt to establish an equitable relationship in the initial stages of approach and engagement. If you have no choice, pick up the toys with nonthreatening and slow body postures. Do not tower over her and keep your body curved and sideways. If she will not take food treats, try leaving a tidbit in the spot of each toy as you remove it.

Be aware of individual dog preference in treats, toys, movement, voice level, and interaction. Watch for tenseness, aggravation, fear, or pain reactions. Read each dog and never assume all dogs like the same approach. Stay flexible in your attempts to bring the dog closer for interaction.

INITIAL AND EARLY STAGES OF CONTACT

When the dog is ready, she may approach for more food or another toy and slow hand contact can start. Hands should be kept low for strokes. Do not go over the animal until she shows she is ready. When the dog does not cringe, run away, or shudder with touch, she is ready to move into actual strokes.

It is important that she associates your hands with good things. This will make handling and training much less frightening in time. Meals should be hand fed in the initial stages of habituating fearful dogs to human presence. A hungry animal will be more highly motivated to face her fear and will learn that human hands deliver resources, two essential elements in socialization by habituation.

When the dog is ready to be touched, read the type of touch she prefers. Most dogs, especially insecure ones, hate pats and slaps. Most prefer stroking that mimics their mother's tongue licks. Light, feathery or fast touches communicate your insecurity, so firm, slow, and gentle strokes will communicate confidence and experience. Do not overwhelm her with your hands wandering everywhere. Desensitize one area of her body at a time.

Because dogs can be left-sided or right-sided, preferring contact on that side, you should limit touch to one side at a time and gradually habituate the dog to touch on both sides. Flitting around from one side to the other with no discernible pattern can upset some dogs.

Your bent elbows, lowered shoulders, and tilted head show lack of aggressiveness in dog language. Entice the dog to come near with treats and a high-pitched encouraging voice. Head contact should be avoided; dogs fear obstruction of their eyes. Blink your own eyes. Blinking is a subliminal, nonthreatening way to look at a dog. Never pat a dog on her head. It is uncomfortable for the dog and makes you vulnerable to a hand bite. Familiarity will eventually allow more head contact. Most dogs eventually enjoy chin and throat scratches. These are areas she cannot easily reach herself.

Most dogs hate gloves, so use a naked hand to touch her if it is safe. Warm your hands so she does not receive the shock of freezing touch. This is especially important with short-haired dogs and dogs with no undercoat. Be careful of static shocks. Try to use hand lotion and start contact when the dog is on a hard surfaced floor, not carpeting. You can even try rubbing stinky canned dog food on your hands to entice her forward and condition her to associate your human scent with the smell of something desirable. Later, when she has accepted your hands, you can discontinue dog-food hand lotion.

More areas of the dog's body can be included as touch desensitization progresses. Watch for pulling away, skin shuddering, strikes with forepaws, mouthing, or head turns. These body language clues display discomfort, and you have either gone too far too fast or have hit a sensitive spot. Respect her request and give her a break from contact. Wait for her to return voluntarily. Positive signs that she enjoys touch are relaxed body, slow tail wags, and sighs.

Just like human parties, it is always better to leave before you have been asked to. Frequent, short sessions of touch are more effective than imprisoning the dog for an hour-long lesson, in which she becomes restless and associates your effort as a source of aggravation. When you stop a session, sit quietly for a moment and then slowly leave the dog. Never shoot straight up and stomp to the door. Aggressive, hurried body language at the end of a quiet, safe encounter will destroy everything you just did.

Instruct all others who come in physical contact with your dog. You will need to habituate your dog to allow her veterinary and grooming needs to be met. These professionals appreciate your guidance and will follow your instructions. If they do not, they can harm the progress you have made. Do not be shy about standing your ground in how you wish your pet to be handled. But habituate her to you first, before she must face strangers. Go slow at first and add new areas of her body and new amounts of pressure with each session.

COLLARING AND LEASHING

When your dog is tolerant of touching, quietly snap a cloth collar on. Never use choke chains on fearful (or any other) dogs. Do not go over her head with the collar or your reach. Scratch her chest, neck, and withers. When she tolerates your hands in those areas, you can slip one end of the collar under her throat and snap it in back of her neck, never under her ear (because the noise may startle her). A touch of oil lubricant beforehand will make the snap-on sections go together with less noise.

Snap-on collars are safer than buckle collars because immediate release is critical if the dog ever becomes entangled. Buckle collars take too long to release and are difficult to maneuver when a choking, panicked dog is flailing about. Make sure the collar is loose enough to avoid causing her alarm but tight enough that she cannot get a paw entangled in it. Two flattened fingers should easily slide between her neck and the collar.

Bend to attach her leash from her side, with your body sideways, also. Bending directly in front of the dog will place your body in a vulnerable position. A nervous dog may jump up into your face for a bite or a submissive kiss. If that happens, your balance will be compromised, causing you to tumble backwards with the force of the forward moving dog's weight. You are in a safer position if you leash from the side.

Avoid fast movements. Keep a solid, sideways stance. That way, you can keep your position and will not need a sudden off-balance leg adjustment if the dog does jump up or shies away. Dogs, especially those who have been kicked, are wary of legs and feet. Deliberate leg and foot movements are hugely important because they are the first parts of the human body a dog can see, as well as the parts of the human body closest to dog level. Small dogs are doubly aware of feet and legs.

Once leashed, the dog is ready to move on to being groomed, a more advanced type of touch.

GROOMING

Grooming is an excellent way to bond with your dog, teach her to trust, and physically relax her, as well as an excellent way to examine the condition of her skin, coat, ears, eyes, mouth, and feet. Begin where initial touch left off, using the same pressure and speed of hand movement.

The dog should be on a short leash but not tightly restrained. Keep the leash looped around your wrist so your hands are free for gentle handling. A six-foot leash will keep her close but allow her to move away when she is overwhelmed. Allow periodic moving away. The dog is attempting, on her own, to avoid going over threshold. Let her move only to the length of the leash to learn she has some power to move away but will not be reinforced by full avoidance. Encourage her to reengage and approach again. Praise should follow her return to you, not heavy-handed correction for lack of attention.

Next, introduce a soft brush by allowing her to see and smell it. Let her move to the brush for investigation; do not shove it into her face. Slowly move the brush to her body and follow the same path with your opposite hand in lengthy strokes. The dog may respond with curiosity, slight discomfort, or insecurity. If you have moved slowly enough, she should not get up and run. With each hesitation, reintroduce the brush to her sight and nose.

Be aware of static shocks that occur in dry conditions. Static can build up in a brush and the dog's coat. Static shocks are negative experiences that will defeat your desensitization goals. Antistatic laundry sprays can be applied to the brush to eliminate static in the air or on the brush. When using them, apply them before the brushing session and spray away from the dog. Sprays can frighten the dog and/or make it hard for the sensitive dog nose to breathe. Portable humidifiers can also be placed in the training area, and fabric softener sheets can be stroked over a longhaired dog to control deeper electrical charges in a thick, dense coat.

When the dog is comfortable with one brush, another tool can be introduced the same way. Introduction of a new tool may happen in the first grooming session, or it may have to wait until the next one. Again, watch for hesitation and comfort level in the dog. Choose a softer version of a tool if she is emaciated or if she has mats, injuries, or other impediments to smooth-flowing brushes.

Be careful how much pressure you exert. Do not fight to pull out burrs or mats. Cut them out, but only when you are confident that she will hold still enough to allow safe removal without injury.

Grooming at this stage is not for appearance. It may take months of slow, step-by-step work to remove all mats and tangles, but it is better to take the time than rush the dog and end up with an unsatisfactory experience. If large chunks of hair or fur must be left knotted, remember that looks do not matter, but handling and habituation do. All experiences at this time must be pleasant, short, and frequent. They should never put her over threshold for touch tolerance or into painful fear reaction. Confinement used for grooming may cause claustrophobic stress, even when you are simply keeping her close by leash. Give the dog frequent breaks to move around, break contact, and come back. Shorter, more frequent grooming sessions are better than long, detail-oriented confinements.

Feet are particularly vulnerable areas for dogs. Handling her feet should begin slowly and only after other areas of her body are entrusted to your touch. Barring any immediate injury or medical condition, feet should be left for last in the desensitization process. Gradual progression to paws and claws may take days or weeks, but positive reinforcement should always precede pulling away. You may have to settle for one toenail clip at a time.

If your dog will not tolerate foot handling, do not fight. Do not let her associate anxiety and negative interactions with you. Take her to a qualified groomer or veterinarian for initial nail care. Safe, professional handling by strangers will save you possible physical injury, save your relationship with your dog, and save your dog from serious emotional injury. It is doubly advantageous if you can find a groomer with fearful dog handling skills.

If handling and grooming are not positive and enjoyable experiences for a fearful pet, there will be slower progress in the relationship. If you experience tension within yourself in anticipation of a struggle with your dog, the dog will be aware of the battle about to ensue. If touch contact is negative for both of you, it defeats the purpose of increased emotional bonding, and building further trust will be impossible. When each handling/grooming session ends, give the dog quiet, happy verbal praise and slowly move away.

MOVEMENT AND CALMING

Many trainers neglect habituating a dog to human movement. Dogs learn quickly how to interpret body language and can be frightened by what they perceive as aggressive action. All movement around fearful dogs should be calm, quiet, slow, and relaxed.

People greet each other in enthusiastic straight-on approaches. They make direct eye contact, smile, and quickly reach out for handshakes. A dog's view of a polite greeting will be the opposite of how humans greet one another. Be mindful of how a dog sees you in her own world of body language. Curved approaches, softened body postures, sloped shoulders, indirect eye gaze, and bent arms with relaxed hands will be less threatening to a dog.

Upright body, head back and up, direct eye contact, shoulders stiff and braced, straight arms, hands spread open, long leg strides, and speed communicate aggression, and those behaviors will frighten insecure dogs who are inexperienced with normal human body language.

Fearful dogs can be calmed by appropriate movements as well. If a dog is on the edge of a fear reaction, she will look to you for guidance if she trusts you. Fearful movement in dogs and people is fast, short, and jerky. Fearful breathing will consist of gasps, pants, snorts, or huffs. With slow, confident body posture and movement, controlled breathing, and a cheerful yet quiet voice, you can calm an upset dog. If she sees no flight or fight (fear or aggression body language) in you, it will reassure her.

Study your dog and find what her own relaxed physical behavior looks like. Mimicking her can result in a mutual language and build nonthreatening rapport.

Mirror and Displacement Activity

A humorous example of "mirroring" body language was in an episode of *Hot in Cleveland,* a television series about four women from Hollywood. On their way to Paris to escape various life misfortunes, they are forced to land in Cleveland, Ohio, when the plane develops mechanical problems. They decide to stay in Cleveland. One of the characters, actress Victoria Chase, receives a visit from her alienated daughter who has written a tell-all book about her mother. Victoria announces to her roommates that to establish empathetic rapport with her daughter, she will engage in an actor's skill called mirroring. She explains that she will mirror or mimic the body language of her daughter. The daughter is also an actress and catches on to the ploy. The result is a hilarious vision of two vain, controlling women copying each other's movements with increasingly competitive exaggeration to outdo each other.

Although this use of mirroring was used comically, when used subtly, it is a valuable tool in helping fearful dogs overcome their discomfort in the presence of people. Socialized dogs read us even when we are not aware of what we project with our arms, legs, facial expressions, and postures. They sense our tension, smell anger in our body secretions, and see sadness in our facial expressions. Yet, few people make the effort to observe and copy dog body language, which can bring comfort to a fearful dog and increase communication with her. By casually copying the body movements of your unsure dog, the dog may calm herself in your presence.

In her popular book, *On Talking Terms With Dogs: Calming Signals,* author Turid Rugaas describes body actions that dogs use to calm themselves and others. She states that yawning belies stress, licking lips shows tension, and averted eyes shows deference. She says if we mimic our dogs' actions, we will calm them because we are speaking their language.

To lessen their tension, dogs will also engage in displacement activities. In an effort to establish dog-to-dog nonthreatening harmony, they do "dog things" like casual sniffing and peeing on bushes while watching what another dog nearby does. The secondary dog—the dog being watched—will copy the displacement activity of the first. This shows peaceful intent. Following displacement activity, nonaggressive dogs will approach each other in a curved and nonchalant path.

To take on the role of the secondary dog, you can copy your dog's behavior as you walk with her. Stop when she stops, walk when she walks. Mimic panting, sniffing, sighing, and other dog behavior to put an anxious dog at ease. To avoid an appearance of "stalking," keep your body in softened postures: sideways from the dog, no direct eye contact, relaxed shoulders and hands, small steps, and unhurried movements.

These tiny, yet time-consuming steps establish important first contact. Gentle and peaceful presence can begin the long climb to trust.

Habituating and Mirroring with a Feral Dog

The most extreme fearful dog case I have worked with was a feral pit bull mix named Skittles. She courageously faced anything in her life—except people. She was deathly afraid of touch, eye contact, the slightest movement of feet, hands, and any posture or movement that faced her straight on.

I spent months feeding Skittles stinky canned dog food (appealing to a formerly starved dog) by hand. In the beginning of her habituation training, I had my own three dogs join in our sessions. Skittles stood far off, watching my dogs enjoy the rarity of canned food, and was mesmerized by their happily taking food right out of my hands. When she decided to join in, I remained still, held out food in the flat palm of my hand, and looked away as she approached. It took time for her to take the food and she never touched my hand, just pulled the food from my palm with her lips. When each piece was in her mouth, Skittles immediately backed away, ready to run. With time, she backed up less and less distance. Eventually, she stopped backing up and even let her tongue and muzzle brush my palm.

After success in feeding Skittles by hand, I placed my dogs on stay commands at a distance while I enticed Skittles to come closer to me. They received food less frequently, but their presence reassured the still skittish Skittles.

Eventually, I worked only with Skittles. When my own dogs were banned from her lessons, I placed food on my body parts that she was afraid of. I laid chunks of food on my knees, on my toes, and held it next to my eyes, while looking down. Skittles tilted her head in curiosity but would not come all the way forward. Slowly, I took each piece and I handed them to her. Each session I shortened my reach, and she came closer to my body in order to gulp food from my fingers.

Once she became comfortable with this, I left the food chunks on my feet or knees instead of handing them to her. To get the food, she had to retrieve it from the feared body part. She dodged in, hastily grabbed the food, then jumped back, and swallowed. She retreated slower and less distance as the days wore on. Finally Skittles eagerly ate chunks of food from my toes, knees, thighs, hands, and even took pieces from my fingers held next to my downcast eyes.

When Skittles habituated to my unmoving individual body parts, I held food out to her while I moved my feet, legs, hands, and torso ever so slightly. She mastered taking food from my moving hand, while my body gently gyrated. I began small movements of my toes and knees, while the food lay on top. I placed the food directly on my sliding feet and slowly bouncing knees. Once again she jumped back but eventually accepted the small swings of my toes and knees, and gulped the food.

One morning she did not retreat. Boldly her eyes tried to anticipate where I would place a chunk and she waited for my next offering. I knew we had turned her fear of my body into a game of "Where will the food be next?" When *she guessed right—I often rigged her to be right—I gave her a jackpot reward of more than one chunk and verbally praised her courage. I kept my voice high-pitched, sing-song, and playful. This dog was young and did enjoy the game once she realized I would not hurt her.*

Next, I held chunks in various positions and heights around her head and waited for her to reach for it. Skittles learned that voluntary approach and closeness to all parts of my body in her own various positions were safe and rewarding fun. Although it took months, Skittles eventually accepted eye contact with me, learned to enjoy walks on a leash and ball games in the yard, and finally came to appreciate the touch of grooming.

During our months together, I mirrored Skittles and my other dogs around the house and in the yard so she could understand that I was an accepted member of the pack. I felt silly sometimes, but I had to pull from every-thing I knew about behavior modification and experiment to save this dog's life. We succeeded. She was adopted and remains with owners who were willing to learn how to live with her. Under their tutelage, she continues to improve.

VOICE AS A TOOL

Effective use of your voice as a tool is as important as collars, leashes, food, toys, or environmental controls. Pairing vocal sounds with all physical activities around fearful animals augments other habituation attempts. Consistent, monotonic sound calms, yet does not interfere with activity. Calming sound will augment calming movement.

White Noise Humming

I have discovered that the use of tonal humming can lull a fearful animal and habituate her to the sound of the human voice. Dogs who have had limited or no exposure to people can become overwhelmed with our constant verbal chatter and our confusing complexity of sound variations. During initial habituation, slow and deep to medium level humming can relax a fearful pet. Humming gives a fearful dog an audible location as you move around her or when you are out of her sight. That will prevent her from being startled when you suddenly appear around a corner or in a doorway.

Silent presence throws animals back to the limbic fear of being stalked as prey by larger predators, even if they themselves are a predatory species. Monotonic humming is a form of verbal displacement activity that reduces that primal fear in animals not accustomed to human closeness.

Research has been done to determine which audio tones and which decibels increase relaxation, aid learning, or bring about deep sleep. White noise machines reproduce tones that accomplish these goals. I discovered that low tone humming around fearful animals appears to have the same effect. It relaxes a tense dog body during grooming, allows the animal to locate me with minimal disruptive movement, and calms stress hormones so she can be around me without anxiety.

What I have come to call white noise humming does not have to be actual music. A dog does not know Mozart from the Beatles. Nonsensical humming is adequate. Most important are the tonal level and the speed of note change. Attention should be paid to the response of the dog. The appropriate level of tone, volume, and pattern of the hum will accomplish relaxation.

Word chatter does not seem to accomplish the same relaxation as melodic humming. I believe this is because when people speak to a dog, they unconsciously put focus on the dog through eye contact and body language. Timid dogs do not enjoy being focused on. The body posture, direct eye contact, and psychological attention of the speaking human can be intimidating. Humming is an unfocused sideline (displacement) activity with no response expected from the dog. This takes direct attention and pressure off her.

Voice, Intent, and Vocabulary

Human voices can be sources of irritation, comfort, praise, encouragement, correction, or criticism. People have come to depend on verbal communication, and because we are so dependent on language, we expect our pets to understand what we say and how we say it. But it is the tone, speed, and volume that animals process, not our words. Until a dog is trained to understand individual words, she will focus on our overall sounds, not specific words or sentences. Yet people still believe, "She knows exactly what I'm saying." No other creature or person pays as much attention to you as your devoted dog, but that does not mean she "knows."

When people attribute comprehension of our language to their dogs, they are indulging in one aspect of "anthropomorphism." Anthropomorphism is the term used to refer to the unrealistic assignment of human emotional and cognitive interpretations to animals. It is not helpful to believe our dogs understand what we say or to believe we understand what our dogs are thinking.

Although animals share many of our primary emotions, we assume that we understand what they are thinking, and these assumptions often cause miscommunication. Many dogs are relinquished or abandoned when people accuse them of the same kinds of emotional manipulations people practice on each other. Research shows that dogs are not capable of high levels of cognitive complexity, especially those based in ulterior motives.

For example, contrary to many people's beliefs, animals do not act out of revenge. The person whose dog pees on her bed when she goes on vacation and leaves him behind, wrongly assumes that her dog has peed on the bed as an act of revenge. Undesirable dog behavior interpreted by human ignorance can lead to rejection of the dog. When a dog's true motivation for a negative behavior is understood, it is often easily remedied. Most negative behavior results from insecurity, fear, or confusion regarding pack (family) balance—all of which can result in anxiety. We have already discussed many forms of dog anxiety but there is another crucial contributor.

Many dogs are sensitive to critical tones of voice. Contempt and disgust are basic emotions that Darwin discovered most animal species share cognitively with humans. Dogs do not understand the *use* of derision but seem able to understand the *negativity* of verbal derisions, such as ridicule, aimed at them. When a dog is ridiculed, he appears to be embarrassed. Dropped head and submissive posture to appease are common reactions to verbal criticism. When dogs sense disapproval, they may cower or slink away, hence the anthropomorphic misconception that "he knew he had been bad." Disdainful verbal criticism is inhumane and pointless. The dog will not associate derision with his own behavior. He will only interpret you as unpredictable, which will lead to more fear—not confidence or trust in you.

Besides tone of voice, dogs can learn to decipher many words, but only through association with nouns (toy, bone, ball) and action (come, go, sit), not in abstract thoughts ("I think, therefore I am."). I had an Australian Shepherd who learned adjectives. He figured out the difference between a "big" stick and a "little" stick. He also had a vocabulary of three hundred words and was able to understand simple complete sentences that I taught him incrementally. But most owners do not invest the immense time it takes to teach their dog such detailed communication.

Barbara Woodhouse, a famous British dog trainer, said that the average dog can learn a vocabulary equivalent to that of a five-year-old child. Few people spend the time or have the knowledge to teach their dog the way they do their child. Yet, even the least genetically intelligent dog becomes fluent in his owner's body language and tones of voice, if not actual words.

How many dogs become excited when owners "think" of leaving the house? Dogs are believed to read minds, but what they are excellent at reading is body language. Departure cues start long before car keys are jangled. There have already been numerous subconscious body language messages to the ever-astute dog. If there is conversation between human household members, dogs easily pick up on voice cues. Voice and unconscious body language provide dogs with more information than people sometimes intend.

Speed and Enunciation

When we speak quickly, our words lace together, and dogs cannot differentiate them individually. Listening to a native French speaker when you have beginner-level comprehension skills makes hearing individual words difficult, and the same is true for dogs who struggle to learn what we say to them. Words should be spoken to dogs slower than used with people in conversation, broken up clearly, and spoken loud enough that the dog can hear but not so loud to cause tension.

Enunciation is important when teaching command words. Clear pronunciation and consistent use of the same command words for behaviors will help the dog understand. Once the dog becomes capable of performing a chain of commands (a series of actions resulting from minimal command words), it is more imperative to clearly pronounce each word in the sentence intended to provide behavioral direction.

Volume

Volume variety is part of the extensive verbal repertoire humans have evolved to communicate with each other. Although dogs use volume variety on occasion, human usage is far more complex.

Extreme volume levels, from bellowing orders to murmuring endearments, can confuse and frighten dogs who are unfamiliar with human complexities in voice usage. Loudness can lead to fear and avoidance. Medium volume can comfort and encourage association. Whispering can frighten shy dogs who are sensitive to the sensation of silent predatory approach. These primitive instincts still reside in the amygdala, even though a dog may never have been hunted by a predator. Finding the optimal level of voice to communicate with and comfort an anxious dog will be a matter of trial and error.

I advise you to save loud volume for emergency commands. And even when there is urgency for an animal to cooperate, such as calling a dog away from an oncoming car, *calmness must remain within the volume* or your anxiety will raise his. Raised anxiety will cause stress hormones to shut down the dog's cognitive functioning. He may freeze or run away from your rising voice, which may be exactly the opposite of the behavior you need at that moment.

Also, do not increase volume in a repetitious staccato of a command ("Sit. Sssit. *SIT!*"). You may hope that with each increase in volume and speed, the dog will finally realize you are serious, but this will not work as you intend it to. It can backfire if the timid dog finds your loudness intimidating. He will freeze in fear, not perform the desired behavior.

People even yell at each other if they feel the person spoken to does not understand. I am always amazed and entertained by someone trying to give directions in their own language to a foreign visitor. When the visitor has difficulty understanding the unfamiliar language, the speaker raises his volume, as if by being louder, the strange words will suddenly make sense.

If a dog does not respond to a normal or even a quiet request for a behavior, wait and let the animal think. If the dog still does not seem to understand the request, lead him to a rewardable response with basic dog training skills. Start over in your approach to teaching the word your dog does not comprehend. Yelling only raises a dog's anxiety and blocks logical thinking. A frightened dog will not engage in problem solving or even try to guess what you want. He may just shut down and give up.

Tone

Tone is another aspect of the human voice that is an important tool in working with animals, particularly fearful ones. Softness or firmness of tone can easily transmit your intent. Unthreatening soft tones will communicate safety, comfort, and respect.

High-pitched tones are often playful, affectionate levels that dogs respond to. The human tendency to "baby talk" animals does not seem to help or deter communication; the high-pitched tone that accompanies it has more influence.

Medium conversational tones can communicate that it is time to work/learn. They can also communicate your role as leader and help a pet feel secure. Saying "Come, let's get busy," or "Time to work, buddy," in a confident everyday tone will entice a dog to take his place at your side for companionship.

Firm, deep vocal tones impart stern intent as in a correctional noise marker, like, "Eh, eh, eh!" These tones should cause an animal to cease behavior and look for redirection. Then the tone should immediately return to a common medium tone for redirection of command. Following that, switch again to high-pitched praise for the dog's successful performance of the new behavior.

For example, if your dog sniffs something questionable on a walk, instead of jerking his neck with the leash, say, "Eh-eh, leave it!" in a firm, semi-loud tone. When he looks up to you in surprise say, "Come," in a medium conversational tone, re-directing his attention once he gives it to you. When your dog moves toward you, immediately raise your tone to a sing-song, "Good job! What a good puppy!"

The human voice can cover a large range of tones and volume with practice. Men must learn to raise their voices and women should conquer lowering theirs. Emotional and tonal control is essential to training, particularly with fearful dogs, who are often predisposed to ultra-sensitivity to the slightest variations of sound. You can be more careless in volume and tone usage with a confident, one-owner trained Great Dane than with a fearful, unsocialized, rescued puppy mill Chihuahua.

Voice control is a stepping-stone in learning to control emotion. Where one goes, so goes the other. Emotion and voice are intertwined, and though animals cannot decipher complex meanings, they are quick to interpret what they see and hear.

DOVETAILING VOICE, EMOTION, AND TRAINING

Fearful, timid, and shy dogs are extremely sensitive to human body postures, eye contact, and voice usage. People are overly involved with verbal communication and do not pay attention to their other forms of communication, which dogs read by nature. Emotions in people flow fluently into all aspects of their physical appearance, movements, and sounds, although they are rarely sensitive to what they are subliminally saying to their dog.

All of these human peccadilloes will affect every aspect of communication between you and your dog student. If you work with fearful dogs, know that they, more than other canine personality types, are extraordinarily sensitive and acutely aware of your moods, probably even before you are. Establishing a relationship of trust with an unsure dog will require possibly exhausting effort on your behalf to be consistently aware of how you appear, sound, and express yourself.

A dog's eyes will constantly be on you, watching. His ears will be tuned to you and his brain will be interpreting your every move. He will interpret you as he interprets other canines. If he has been abused, neglected, or treated cruelly by people in the past, he will be far more aware and wary. Prior mixed messages from people will have left him on edge and more prone to confusion. Therefore, your human emotions must be tightly controlled during every encounter with your frightened friend.

CHAPTER 11

━╱┃╲━

Training the
Fearful Dog

The effective trainer controls personal emotion, except for compassion. Anger, frustration, ego, and the need for power must be abandoned. When your patience runs thin, anger begins to flow, and frustration seeps into your voice and attitude. This is the time to end the training session.

Always finish on a positive note. If the dog stops making progress, go back to the last rewardable behavior, ask for the performance, praise him, and quit. Keep your emotions cheerful and encouraging, even if it is difficult.

It can be hard to stop at the right time because no trainer wants to feel like a failure. Your ego should remain fluid and your attitude humble. The dog seeking to understand is honoring you with his attention and trust. When your feelings of superiority over the unknowing dog dominate your training, you and he are in real trouble.

EMOTIONAL AND EGO CONTROL IN TRAINING

Arrogant trainers become rigid in their approaches. They often become frustrated when a timid dog does not adhere to the time frame for progression that the trainer expects. Arrogance blinds a trainer to each dog's individuality—both strengths and weaknesses—because it blinds the trainer to their own strengths and weaknesses. To work with dogs is to work on self-control.

However, a healthy ego is needed to be a leader. You need courage to plan a course of behavior modification without knowing if your plan will succeed—and you cannot know if it will succeed until you implement the plan. You also need to be flexible enough to alter course when necessary. But too great an ego can tie your problem-solving ability to inefficient, outmoded, or unkind techniques. Ego and arrogance combine in close-minded ignorance, and there is no worse combination in a trainer.

A strong leader will assist the fearful dog in improving his self-confidence. The dog must also have confidence in his human leader for protection and advocacy as he attempts to navigate his way through his life with people. A strong leader will also help the dog develop the ability to independently assess whether fear is an appropriate response to a situation and what, if any, action is needed. You can teach the dog how to cope by self-stress reduction and through logical reasoning. Your dog can learn to seek safe places, look to you for your reaction, and recognize stimuli that were previously new and alarming. With your help, he will eventually control his own fear reactions. Even if he remains unsure in any scenario, you will see less knee-jerk limbic panic, and counteraction that is more purposeful. Observing your dog pass cognitively from primitive amygdala-caused startle to cerebral cortex reasoned reaction will show you that your dog is ready to progress in his behavior modification program.

However, progress can be halted and sometimes regressed, by an impatient, insensitive trainer. The most hurtful and disastrous trait in a trainer is the need for power. Animal abuse and cruelty has been perpetrated on countless dogs in the name of training that was only a disguise for addiction to power. Tantrums, yelling, ridicule, and physical punishment have no place in any type of dog training, but especially not in working with dogs who are already insecure around, and afraid of people.

If you lack sufficient equanimity in thought and/or emotions, and if you are inconsistent in your treatment of your dog, his trust will never be fully established. Dogs are also excellent judges of insincerity. They can comprehend inauthenticity, even if they cannot intellectually label it. Knowledgeable flexibility in training methods must be accompanied by stable emotional control. Taking a fearful dog under your wing has special idiosyncracies you must be aware of and willing to face.

CORRECTION AND REDIRECTION

Training a fearful dog can be tricky. Precautions must be taken to prevent the dog from associating fear with learning. It is possible that the dog was previously treated with heavy-handed attempts to train, which may account for his timidity. Some fearful dogs have never had much contact with people and so have no history in the close bond that can develop between dogs and people who trust each other. Guiding an insecure dog to skills and behavior that will make him easier and more pleasant to live with can be complex and trying at times.

One of the main reasons training insecure dogs can be a challenge is that a fearful pet cannot be corrected in the early stages of learning. No correction should be used until the dog has thorough knowledge of what is being asked. For a fearful pet, even the slightest hint of disapproval can send him into panic. Guiding a dog from a negative behavior to a rewardable one is the best approach for training fearful dogs. Rewards and encouragement must be your tools; if you cannot provide those because the behavior of the dog is not something you want to encourage, it is best to ignore that undesirable behavior. As my grandmother used to teach, "If you cannot say anything nice, do not say anything at all."

For example, you should never reprimand any dog for urinating or defecating in the house if the dog is not caught in the act. Unless corrected *during* the undesirable behavior, the dog will have gone on to another behavior and you will be punishing that, not the behavior you meant to punish. Even well-adjusted dogs are incapable of associating previous negative behavior to correction unless they are in the process of performing the behavior when corrected. If a dog is caught lifting his leg on the couch, a loud sound can be made to stop the behavior. For instance, you may use a hand clap or one word, such as, "Hey!"

But if a *fearful* dog is caught urinating on the couch, any sound may startle him and he may have the following knee-jerk reactions. He may urinate harder due to fright—all animals, even humans, lose control of bodily functions when certain fear levels are reached. He may run away and not trust you again, thanks to what he will view as the unpredictable nature of your fury. Perhaps worse, he may do both of these things at the same time, leaving a trail of uncontrolled urine wherever he runs.

So how *do* you correct a fearful dog at the beginning, before he learns to trust that correction does not mean painful punishment?

Unfortunately, for urination and defecation you cannot make any noise to stop the behavior. Instead, walk towards the dog. That is usually enough to stop elimination due to his building insecurity at the straight-on approach. The dog will freeze, at which time you can cheerfully entice him outside or encourage him to go out the dog door before it is his decision (to avoid reinforcing escape behavior). This will stop the dog's activity and quickly cut off budding panic by your cheerful redirection of behavior. A quiet, straight-on approach also works to put a temporary stop on other undesirable behaviors as well, but it must be followed by cheerful redirection so the dog does not view you as a confusing stalker.

Leave scented rags from your inside cleanup job outdoors to subliminally guide the dog to the proper place for elimination. Pick up poop from the indoor errors and place it in the area of the yard you want the shy dog to learn to use. This will accomplish two things. First, it will pre-scent the outside to encourage regular visits. Second, it will teach the dog that one area of the yard is the preferred location for elimination, which will eventually make yard poop scooping more expedient for you. Dogs often pick the places they prefer and naturally stick to that area, so you can encourage him to train himself to *your* preferred area. It will also give the dog confidence in routine—same place, same activity. Open spaces like yards can intimidate shy dogs, so having a regular potty zone reinforces his security in "his" territory, making him more likely to develop the habit of returning for elimination. Make sure you also deodorize the inside area to discourage a repeat performance.

For dogs who show great fear at straight-on approaches, it is best to ignore the negative behavior. Instead of responding to the negative behavior, immediately attempt to bait the dog into a desirable, rewardable behavior. For example, if your fearful dog dumps over the trash, offer a tasty treat to pull him away from the mess. Use the treat to distract the dog into a sit command, then happily reward him. Slowly return to the mess and clean it up (always use slow movements with a fearful dog, and also control your own frustration.). Make sure to place the trash where the dog cannot have access to it (which you should have anticipated to begin with). Always help animals succeed by thinking ahead and removing access to possible undesirable behavior motivators.

THE MOST IMPORTANT COMMAND

Coming on command is the most important lesson every dog should learn. It is an especially important skill for a timid dog. Because fearful dogs are almost always flight risks, accomplishing the challenge of a reliable recall can save you and your timid friend days and possibly weeks of turmoil when such a frightened dog wanders the streets in panic, too afraid to go to people.

Immediate, enthusiastic, and voluntary approach can save the dog's life in many ways. Coming to you on command may take her out of danger, especially when she has no way of knowing she is vulnerable. When you see danger before your dog does, keep control of your own emotion, body, and tone of voice to avoid premature danger alert. Your own panic can drive her away in sudden fear, perhaps into the danger. Requests for approach must always be calm, cheerful, and positive. Playful recall (return to you on request) is more successful than panicked recall.

When initiating recall training, make it fun, rewarding, and of higher value (lots of yummy treats) than any other activity (chasing squirrels). Coming to you should be so positive an experience that the dog will respond one hundred percent of the time. If your dog hesitates before coming when you call her, up the reward ante. Randomize food treats, use different squeakies, run away from her to entice her to chase—anything and everything to bring her in—should be tried. The goal is to make coming to you on command an automatic, non-thinking, and quick response.

Playful training of recalls will instill a conditioned response in your dog, so when the situation is not playful and lighthearted, but an actual emergency, your dog will not think; only run to you. When your fearful dog learns to recall reliably, both you and the dog will benefit. You will not have to undergo the frustrating process of catching the dog and the dog will not experience the fear of being chased down. You will be assured knowing you can pull your dog out of danger if necessary. Both of you will feel an increased bond of affection and trust when she can rely on your upcoming praise and you can rely on her coming to you by choice. Practice your body language and voice control so you appear welcoming, even in emergency situations.

Never call a dog to you to be chastised. If she is engaged in an undesirable behavior, go to her for redirection of activity. Your body language should be controlled and purposeful, and it should not be a source of fear for her. Once voluntary approach is lost, it can be irretrievable.

When a dog voluntarily approaches you, she shows trust, affection, and willingness to enter the physical realm of relationship. Reward her for approaching by verbal or hand cue, paired with a reward (such as verbal praise, an affectionate touch, food, or a toy). Make coming to you when you call the absolute best, most fun, and fantastic experience she can have. Meticulous and repetitive recall practice is important to keep the action reliable. Never take it for granted that you will always be her highest priority.

Most importantly, unless you have one hundred percent recall reliability, *never* let a fearful dog off leash. Coming on command is imperative for skittish dogs. If your bond is not tight, she may fall into a panicked flight response during an unforeseen scenario. You will not be able to catch her if she is truly in terror. If your dog is not able to reason through her fear from amygdala-based hysteria to cerebral cortex reasoning keep her leashed and safe at your side at all times. Do not take chances. Some dogs never reach off-leash reliability. Accept this reality if your dog is one. It is not a reflection on your skill as a trainer, nor as an indicator of her intelligence. Some dogs are bred with hardwired reactivity that can never be completely altered.

Despite on or off leash reliability, teach your dog to also go to strangers who call her. Countless frightened dogs escape and do not approach good Samaritans who could offer safe haven. Just as coming to you, her trusted leader, is important, so is teaching your timid dog to go to kind strangers. If she is ever parted from you and wandering afraid in a strange place, a stranger may be her lifesaver. Take time to teach your dog to go to all people who call. The odds of her being called by a person with negative intentions is far less likely than her being called by someone who wants to help her if she becomes lost. The fearful dog must be taught that all people are givers of positive resources. She must learn that food, shelter, and safety can be found with any person, not just you.

TRAINING TOOLS FOR UNDESIRABLE BEHAVIORS IN A FEARFUL DOG

Tools to avert your dog from undesirable behaviors can be used in training your fearful dog, and they can be used even when you are not there to supervise.

Static mats are excellent remote (not associated in the dog's mind to you) training tools. These are clear plastic sheets loaded with tiny electrodes. They can be plugged into electrical outlets or operated with batteries. Various sizes are useful for preventing counter surfing (searching for food on the kitchen counters) and door dodging (running out without permission—a big problem with fearful dogs). These mats can be used in numerous scenarios where undesirable behaviors involve the dog's feet. The electrodes produce tiny shocks like the static shock your finger feels when you touch a doorknob after walking on carpet. They are humane and not painful, only surprising. Because the plastic sheet is see-through, it is difficult for a dog to notice it on top of a counter, on the floor, or placed across a piece of furniture. The correction from this type of tool prevents the dog from connecting you to an unpleasant sensation.

When a dog learns that he is only corrected for behavior when you are present, he will engage in the behavior when you are gone. If he is corrected when you are out of sight, he will learn to never engage in that behavior, due to consistent negative consequences. Best of all, he will not associate the correction with you, which maintains his trust. Fearful dogs are especially sensitive to handler-based physical correction.

To successfully correct undesirable behavior without a trainer in sight, the correction must fit three criteria. 1) It must be remote and not attributable to the trainer. 2) It must be strong enough to stop the behavior. 3) It must work 24/7 without fail. None of these criteria can be reliably fulfilled by a human trainer. If the correction does not work one hundred percent of the time, the correction will become randomized and ineffective.

For example, fearful dogs easily become nuisance barkers. Yelling at any dog to stop barking does not work. Insecure dogs bark to establish distance between themselves and a feared stimulus. Once a dog learns she can drive away a scary person or some other uncomfortable stimulus, barking will become a habit. The best way to avoid habitual nuisance fear barking is to avoid placing the dog in a frightening environment unattended.

Anti-bark machines fulfill all three criteria for correction and do not further frighten fearful dogs. They are humane and effective for most dogs in most situations. Machines come in sonic (audible to humans) and ultrasonic (inaudible to humans but audible to dogs) models. Some operate with batteries (which must be closely monitored so they remain effective) or plug into standard 110V electrical outlets. These devices emit an obnoxious high decibel squeal when barking commences and immediately shut off when barking ceases. Many adjust to allow a designated number of barks before the squeal is triggered.

Crates are another good tool. Desensitizing and habituation of a shy dog requires constant vigilance and presence. That is why crate training fearful dogs is helpful. No owner or trainer can be with the dog constantly, so when absence is necessary, placing the dog in her crate (providing she has been conditioned to know the crate is a safe place) removes the dog's fear when she is left alone. Consequently, panic behavior (separation anxiety and similar phobic behaviors) does not take root in the dog's psyche.

Remote behavioral tools help you maintain a fearful dog's trust while accomplishing correction in a humane way. They also help to avoid negative behavior in the first place.

CORRECTION CUES

Correction cues can be used safely without causing fear. Most humane correction cues used for training between a dog and her teacher are noise markers. Use of noise or silence can stop an undesirable behavior and encourage a fearful dog to look to you for redirection. When the correction cue is used and the dog stops the behavior and voluntarily looks for redirection instead of fleeing, great steps in learning can take place.

Noise Markers

Noise markers are specific sounds used in training for purposes of correction or reward. Noise markers used as correction tools can be vocal sounds, physical sounds, or a combination of the two. The purpose of any noise marker is to cause the dog to stop what she is doing (a behavior you do not want her to do) and to look to you for further guidance. During her brief cessation of activity, you must happily show her an alternative behavior and reward her when she does it.

Voice markers like, "Eh, eh, eh," "Stop," or "Hey!" are vocal markers. Do not confuse the use of an instructional verbal marker with yelling at your dog. Yelling at a fearful dog will frighten her and erode her trust, slowing further training progression, and damaging your relationship. Second, only yelling and not following up with further instruction teaches the dog to either run away from or ignore you. Neither of these consequences is a goal in working with your timid student.

Physical sounds can also serve as markers. Physical sounds you produce at the proper moment for correction include hand claps or leg slaps (on your own leg), whistles, and slaps of a rolled up paper against your knee or hand. You can also place coins in a can and shake them or throw them in the direction of a dog about to do something unacceptable. For instance, a can with coins gently tossed near her can be used to teach a dog the "leave it" command when she is about to eat something questionable and she is not close enough for you to bait away with a treat. Physical corrections not paired with your immediate redirection of the dog to rewardable behavior do not work and will only confuse her.

Voice markers paired with physical markers will escalate the emphasis on urgency to stop a behavior. Combining an "Eh-eh-eh!" with a hand clap should produce enough noise emphasis that a dog will stop a behavior, such as lifting a leg on your couch. Redirection should immediately follow with cheery instruction and praise.

A noise marker must never be used as a punishment, especially with a fearful pet. Use of your hands should be limited to a clap to momentarily stop an unwanted behavior or for physical praise through strokes. Using your hands for hitting the pet will only teach fear; we have already discussed the importance of associating only pleasurable consequences with human hands. Using paper for striking a dog instead of just a slap against your own thigh to stop a behavior is also a pointless punishment. Throwing a can of coins at the dog, instead of a remote toss or shake to draw attention away from an undesirable behavior, is cruel and teaches nothing.

Once the cessation of the behavior occurs and the dog looks to the source of the noise marker, immediate redirection must be attempted. If you do not follow through with redirection, the dog will learn that no consequence is forthcoming. She will learn to ignore you in your subsequent attempts to stop undesirable behaviors. Even timid dogs learn to ignore a stimulus (you making noise) that has no consequence (redirection).

Noise markers should be used at the lowest volume that stops the negative behavior. Do not assume that noise marker correction needs to be loud, especially with a fearful dog. Soft cues can often accomplish the task, and they accomplish it without the risk of a fear reaction. Volume should be escalated only if the dog persists in the behavior.

A secondary noise marker can be incorporated for emphasis when the dog stubbornly persists in the undesired behavior. However, if any fear response begins, you must cease all correction attempts and quickly switch to reassuring sounds and body postures. Remember, a frightened dog cannot think. Or learn.

Gradually increase volume only to the level of effectiveness—stopping the behavior. Sending a dog over threshold with noise markers is possible, and it is often done, but it fails to teach. When the dog learns that a noise marker is a request to cease current behavior and also learns to look for redirection, the volume can be stabilized or lowered.

Clickers and Whistles as Noise Marker Tools

I have deliberately omitted the use of clickers and whistles in this section. In my experience, many fearful dogs have noise sensitivities and are afraid of the loud snap of traditional dog training clickers and the high-pitched shrillness of whistles, even the so-called, "dog whistles" that only dogs hear. Also, inexperienced trainers combine the noises with aggressive appearing body postures such as thrusting their arm and hand out at the dog when they press the clicker, or standing upright with a sharply bent elbow when holding the whistle to their mouth to blow.

Inexperienced people who train with clickers and whistles do not realize that to the naive dog the obnoxious sound is coming from the trainer's hand. The green trainer's clicker hand is pointed directly at the dog, and their whistle is held to their mouth with a hand. Dogs often do not see the actual clicker or whistle but only hear the snap or shriek from the hand. Again, hands should always appear to deliver only positive things.

In combination, the body movements and noise that result from the use of clickers and whistles often cause a sensitive dog to back up or try to get away from what she interprets as incomprehensible aggression from a person she is not sure of. These results are counterproductive and defeat any attempt to eliminate stress so a shy dog can learn. She will only be reinforced in her fears, and will miss the point of whatever behavior you are trying to teach.

In addition, there will be times outside of formal training sessions when you do not have a clicker or whistle handy. You always have your voice and your hands with you. We discuss the intricate use of voice in other sections of this book.

Silence Markers

Silence can be an effective behavior stopper as well. Just as noise can be used as a marker, silence can be used as a marker. It can be another tool in halting undesirable behaviors when teamed with redirection for reward. Used as behavior interference, silence can result in a dog's cessation of an activity. How does silence work to stop an undesirable behavior?

The inherent sociability of dogs causes them to constantly seek connection. When you respond to a behavior with no response, the dog may stop the behavior that is not producing attention. In the activity gap, you can redirect the dog's behavior to a rewardable performance.

Silence alone will not be sufficient to eliminate behavior in the long term, but it can provide breathing space for the dog and you to reconnect, rethink, and re-perform. If silence can provide a halt to an undesirable behavior and give you time to guide the dog to a rewardable one, it can become a valuable training tool.

Your silence can be highly useful when you realize dogs are social and need connection with their leader. Dogs often interpret silence as social isolation, which challenges their inborn need to be part of a group or family. Understanding dog psychology and their inherent instincts will help you use natural means to obtain your behavior goals with the dog you are becoming acquainted with.

USING DOG SOCIAL PSYCHOLOGY TO CORRECT

Many dogs are so needy for human interaction that any interaction is a reward. Positive interaction (verbal praise, food treats) is positive reinforcement. That is, it will increase the likelihood that whatever the dog was doing when the reinforcement was delivered will reoccur. Negative interaction (yelling, hitting) is negative reinforcement. Ironically, it will also increase the likelihood that whatever the dog was doing when the negative consequence happened will reoccur. Your complete withdrawal of interaction, positive or negative, can get a dog's attention like nothing else. Your silence can be tantamount to social isolation, which is the most profound correction a dog can experience.

For example, when your dog runs away with your shoe, chasing and yelling will result in the dog's avoidance of you, usually by gleefully running out of reach. To the dog, it appears you have joined in the game, and your desire for the shoe shows you place a high value on it. Dogs instinctively want what their leaders place high value on, especially if it will get the dog what she really wants—interaction. Your response to the thief may be negative interaction, but it is interaction, nevertheless. Your shoes are rife with odor, so the theft of it should be seen as the compliment it is. Your dog wanted you but was willing to settle for your scent.

Instead of chasing or yelling, turn your back towards the dog. This removes value from the shoe in the dog's eyes because the shoe has value only when it delivers interaction with you. The dog will come to you for engagement. At this point, playfully redirect the dog to a rewardable behavior and reward, like a yummy treat or more appropriate toy. Praise her and cheerfully bait her away from the shoe. If your pack bonding with her has already been achieved, she will have forgotten the shoe because the joy of your company trumps the pleasure of the shoe. When the dog is out of the area, you can retrieve the shoe. If she stubbornly holds on to it, offer a fair "trade" or higher value consequence, such as a favorite treat or toy.

Socially isolated dogs (for example, dogs confined alone to yards, kennels, or cages) can become addicted to negative interaction, since it is usually the only kind they receive. Ironically, they will respond to the negative as enthusiastically as to the positive interaction they rarely receive.

When a fearful dog asks for engagement, the connection of your relationship is ensured. When a timid dog seeks your company, the road to socialization widens to other applications and possibilities.

UNDERSTANDING NONRESPONSE

What if your timid dog wants to be with you but the noise marker does not work? Is she purposefully ignoring you or rebelling? If the dog fails to respond to the noise marker, one of three things may be happening. 1) She has already gone into a freeze mode from fear of the sound. 2) She is captivated in instinctual fascination with the negative behavior or item and cannot hear the correction. 3) She is confused and needs time to think and respond.

Freeze

If the noise marker was too much, too soon, and the dog is already in the midst of a freeze fear reaction, you will need to backtrack to calm her. Lighthearted vocal sounds and softened body language should counter the startling effect of the noise marker. Praise, accompanied by (preconditioned) food treats or toys should distract her from her fear. Hopefully, behavioral redirection can then be attempted. If that does not work, the training session should revert to the last rewardable behavior the dog knows. Once the dog has performed that behavior, reward her and stop the session. For frightened dogs, a playtime with you is an effective way to distract her from fear, reestablish her trust in you, and end the session positively.

Instinctual Fascination

When the dog's attention is hijacked by primitive instinctual behavior, she may not hear or see you. Her intense focus is on the behavior or item she is fascinated with. Examples of mesmerizing instinctual behavior that may appear to cause a dog to ignore requests for behavior include the following:
- Prey Drive—the dog is focused on potential prey. For instance, she may be staring down a rabbit hole after seeing a live creature disappear.
- Curiosity—the dog becomes mesmerized with something, such as a light reflection on the wall.

- Olfactory fascination—The dog picks up a scent and must find the source.
- Play drive—the dog becomes obsessive-compulsive while tail chasing or cannot give up a toy.

That is the time noise marker escalation should be used. The correction must be loud enough to penetrate the dog's concentration, yet care must be given to ensure that she does not find herself in a fearful situation when she snaps out of it.

Often, a trainer will think that the dog is purposely ignoring the correction. When that happens, the trainer's emotions may be flooded by their ego response. The human need for power will cause the trainer to take offense at being ignored, and he may aggressively approach the dog to reproach her. When the trainer is close enough to trigger the dog to snap back to reality, the dog finds an aggressive, angry person stomping towards her. Immediate fear chemicals will cause the dog to flee, which may further infuriate the trainer. When the dog is flooded with stress, and fear sends her over threshold, anything the trainer wished to teach is lost. Redirection will be impossible or unsuccessful.

Confusion

Often when a dog begins to learn how to learn, time must be allowed for him to cognitively process your request and what the appropriate action is. Allowing him time to think is a respectful response.

If the dog is allowed several moments and responds appropriately, you should reward him with spirited praise and jackpot rewards. Jackpot rewards are larger volumes of treats and more enthusiastic verbal and/or physical compliments. Big rewards should accompany large efforts on the dog's behalf. A fearful dog who stays calm, thinks through what is asked, and responds correctly, compliments you because that behavior demonstrates the quality of relationship and trust you have developed.

If the dog has time to think and still appears confused and/or unsure, guide him to the proper response. To reward him for thinking instead of reacting in fear will further build his self-confidence and trust in you. Your patience during his time of confusion and then praise when he figures it out will show he can expect your support during trying times in learning. He will continue to enjoy learning and trust your leadership.

REPETITION FOR FLUENCY

Fluency is the term used to describe a dog's complete comprehension of a specific command (request for a behavior). Dogs do not generalize well, which means that they may learn a behavior in one environment but not transfer that knowledge to a different environment without new learning through repetition. In other words, a dog may know what "sit" means in the kitchen, but he may need to relearn it in the backyard. When the dog truly knows what a sit command is, he will comply in the kitchen, the backyard, the obedience competition ring, or anywhere else.

Once a dog understands and can perform the same behavior regardless of where it is requested, fluency has been achieved. To have achieved fluency, the dog must be able to perform the requested behavior in all scenarios.

The more repetition he experiences and the more success he achieves through behavior request, reward, and new exposures, the more his self-confidence will build.

Your behavior requests to a fearful dog will be successful if the dog has trust and confidence in you, has growing self-confidence due to successful past accomplishments, and has learned that novelty is not frightening, only different.

PROOFING FOR RELIABILITY

Proofing behavior performance is possible only when fluency is achieved. Fluency is proof that the dog understands the command as a stand-alone word or signal, regardless of environmental distractions.

Reliability in the performance of requested behaviors will develop with time, with trust in you, and with recurring positive rewards as consequences. Rewards can change over time and as the dog advances in fluency. Primary reinforcers such as food can become randomized and then faded out. They can be replaced by secondary reinforcers such as physical and verbal praise. When the dog performs a requested behavior simply because you asked, reliability is reached.

Reliability should never be taken for granted. The formerly fearful dog must continue to be protected from his fear triggers whenever possible. The behaviors he has been taught should continue to be reinforced through practice, accompanied by randomized reward of whatever he finds valuable.

Continued practice of known behavior is called "maintenance." At this level of training, randomized rewards will mean more to the dog. He will be more motivated by the uncertainty of reward delivery. Predictable rewards lose their value. (In the human realm, that is why casino slot machines deliver intermittent wins. A slot machine that always gave the player a win or never gave the player a win would be less exciting and therefore less enticing. It is the unpredictability that has value for the player.)

When behaviors are tied together they are called "chains of command." Chains are a series of tasks performed with minimal request words. Events where chains of command are seen include obedience competitions, work with livestock (herding sheep, rounding up cattle), and agility courses. Chains raise self-confidence in fearful dogs because of the increased ability to communicate with you.

Not all dogs have the intellectual capability for complex chains of behaviors. An extremely shy dog may only be capable of learning the next level of exposure to novel stimuli in his everyday life.

But how does a trainer know when it is an optimal time to advance the fearful dog to more advanced work or when to accept him at the level he has accomplished?

STARTLE/RECOVERY RATIOS

Startle/recovery ratios will help determine when to advance training without setting the dog back in behavior modification growth. Startle/recovery is the amount of time between a fear reaction (jump, shy, cringe) and the dog's recovery (return to investigate, smaller distance of flight, return to upright posture). Highly fearful dogs that have not been socialized will have greater startle responses (jump and run, shy and run, cringe and bite) and no recovery (dog is gone or victim is bitten and retreats, then the dog runs).

Habituation, desensitization, and socialization increase the dog's confidence. Secretions of stress chemicals decrease. As the dog's confidence grows, the recovery time from a startle will decrease as well. This illustrates that the dog has the ability to move herself from primitive limbic brain reaction to reasoning with logical evaluation of the situation. The pet has succeeded in conquering her own fear.

Under your leadership, she will learn to evaluate her own situation and develop a reaction based on reasoned sense of empowerment instead of fear. Do not expect startle behavior to completely disappear, but focus on the intensity of the startle, the time between startle and recovery, and the action the dog deems necessary during and following her recovery. When the process shows steady decline in intensity of startle behavior, decrease in recovery time, and less severe action following the startle, advancement in exposure to new stimuli can proceed.

BACKING UP

At any time in a fearful dog's socialization, there may be several occasions for the need to go backward to the last successful behavior. When the pet demonstrates hesitancy in advancement, stop and analyze what caused the plateau.

The hesitancy to advance might have been caused by you if you did not read the animal adequately and approached her fear tolerance threshold.

Alternatively, it might not have been caused by you. Instead, it may be the result of a genetic or biological instability in the hardwiring of the dog's brain function due to breeding, age, health, or injury.

Another possibility is that it could be the result of a specific fear memory (a stimulus that resulted in a lifelong association of fear) that caused the dog extreme discomfort. You may have no way of knowing about this.

And some hesitancy in advancement is caused by completely novel and unexpected events or stimuli that you could not have anticipated.

When a dog falls back into limbic fear reaction (panic) to a stimulus, you must back up training to the last rewardable performance the dog learned. In short and positive training sessions, you should concentrate on reviewing the fluent performance in as many scenarios as possible to rebuild the dog's self-confidence. Then you should set up the dog for exposure at a distance to and/or in the least intensity of the surprise stimulus. Incremental exposures, rewards, and all the basic steps of desensitization and habituation should be started again. Moving forward in exposure should only be done when the dog's startle/recovery regarding the surprise stimulus is under control.

It can be frustrating when advancement in a long-term behavior modification program slows or stops. You must control your own emotions during times of setback or failure. Do not show discouragement or impatience to the dog when backing up is necessary. When you become upset, your own stress hormones will be a scent flag for the ever-sensitive dog. Instead, logically evaluate behavior modification and training protocols and plot new directions. Learning should always be a happy, positive experience for the dog.

Trainer flexibility, both intellectually and emotionally, is imperative to success in fearful dog rehabilitation work.

TRAINER EMOTIONAL FITNESS

Horse trainer Pat Parelli calls trainer ego control "emotional fitness." Physical fitness brings about increased endurance, coordination, mental sharpness and muscular control. Emotional fitness is increased patience, cognitive awareness, intellectual flexibility, mood control, and empathy towards the student animal. These assets supersede anger, desire for power, ego gratification, and frustration.

There cannot be a rigid time line for training. There is no room in fearful pet rehabilitation for an ego-driven trainer. On the other hand, if you have no self-confidence you will not be able to teach confidence to an anxious animal. If you feel a training session is not going well, end the session rather than continuing to teach while accepting subpar performance—in yourself or the dog. End the session with play. Reward the dog and always walk away from success, not failure. Be open to new approaches and creativity in your techniques. Intellectual flexibility and tenacity in your work will eventually end at the optimal level the dog is capable of achieving.

CHAPTER 12

━╱╎╲━

Realistic Evaluation

R ehabilitation of a fearful dog requires two evaluations at the beginning of the dog's time with a
trainer, foster home, or new adoptive home. First,
a complete physical evaluation should be done, followed
by a thorough behavior evaluation.

A physical evaluation is important to rule out any
biological illnesses or incapacities. Often, physical
ailments or injuries can affect behavior. A dog who is
ill or in pain may react fearfully, even if he does not
react fearfully when he is in good health. A veterinarian
should screen the pet before any behavioral evaluations
begin. If illness or injury is present, those concerns must
be addressed, cured, or on their way to healing before
serious looks at behavioral issues can be considered
reliable.

When the dog is placed in a new environment, you must
allow time for the dog to adjust to it. Immediate detailed
behavior analysis will not provide a correct picture while

the dog experiences relocation insecurity. On-the-spot onetime behavioral evaluations do not provide enough information because the dog may behave one way shortly after coming to a new environment and differently once he is comfortable in his surroundings. Allowing time for adjustment will also provide more reliable information about temperament, energy level, and personality traits. Location of placement is also of concern because dogs commonly act differently in the commotion of a shelter than in a foster or adoptive home.

Apart from his medical history and most recent veterinary evaluation, obtain information on his life history, if it is known, and feedback from others who have worked with him. Determine his age and research inherent breed characteristics. Observe his energy level. Take the dog's sex into consideration because a fearful dog will be distracted by sex hormones like estrogen, progesterone, and testosterone, in addition to stress hormones like cortisone and adrenaline. All dogs should be spayed or neutered and sex hormones allowed to dissipate before you do a final behavioral analysis.

THE FIRST WEEK

During the first week of placement, the dog will begin to settle into his new environment. You may see anxiety and energy in the dog that will not reflect his true temperament. Serious behavioral analysis should be postponed, but observance of the dog during this initial time of stress will help you understand what the dog's behavior is in his worst state.

A rigid household or shelter schedule should be established that can be followed during initial stages of desensitization and habituation. This will provide an opportunity for the dog to be comforted by the repetitiveness of routine. It will also help establish a baseline of behavior in a steady routine, which will make behavioral challenges in later routine alterations easier to figure out. Any variance from the new routine during this time will slow his socialization progress until he has developed enough self-confidence in his new situation, and enough trust in you, to begin small departures from routine.

THE SECOND WEEK

You should see calming in the dog during the second week. Extremely anxious dogs, dogs that have not been socialized, and animals rescued from neglect, abuse, or cruelty will take much longer to settle in. But if the daily routine is followed faithfully, the dog will begin to know what to expect. He will learn to look forward to events such as feeding or exercise times.

You should concentrate on companionship at this time and not worry about structured training schedules. You can begin initial analysis of behavioral traits by simple observation. Observe how the dog deals with his food. Does he wolf it down or chew slowly? Observe other behavior. Does he hide? If so, where does he hide? Under things or in deep, dark holes? Does he pace and jump at every sound or does he casually observe while remaining alert to everything? How much companionship and how physically close does he need/want to be? Does he lean into you, follow you from room to room, or does he hang back, eyeing you warily?

Weeks Three and Four

For most dogs, the worst anxiety-motivated behaviors begin to subside or soften in severity during weeks three and four. Again, strict routine should be adhered to. Initial positive reinforcement behavior modification can begin with simple praise for naturally occurring good behavior. Quietly praise the dog for relaxed postures, laying down, making eye contact, calmly walking on leash, or any natural unfearful dog activity that you will eventually want to put on cue (command word). Praise for desirable natural behaviors will provide forward-looking pre-training.

Pairing pre-training with natural exercise (using common command words during walks, for example) gives the dog's nervous brain a chance to concentrate while his body expends excess energy that could distract him from learning. Daily activities such as these also provide valuable repetition opportunities, allowing the dog to learn informally, without effort, in a comfortable setting.

When you live with the dog for a month, obvious personality traits will become apparent. At this point, a more detailed behavioral analysis can be relied on as being realistic. An initial formal training/socialization program can be developed and put into practice.

Also, about this time, resident dogs will begin to adjust to the newcomer as more than just a temporary boarder. Pack juggling will begin. Pack juggling is each dog's attempt to establish his or her position in the group. Former beliefs of rigid wolf pack structure with alphas and omegas, dominance and submissiveness, were once applied to dogs. It is now known that dogs are more fluid in their family relationships, but still some organization must be developed whenever a new canine joins daily life. Allow for this relationship building between animals in the home and interfere only if there is serious conflict.

Recent studies have shown that by the three-month mark, most dog personality traits have become apparent and the dog is generally settled into his new environment. This may vary with highly reactive or extremely shy dogs but for most, three months is the turning point for true settling in.

Getting to Know You

Throughout the initial "getting to know you" stage, routine should be adhered to. Fear stimuli should be observed and avoided, once known. This is the most important time for you to take baseline readings on what fear stimuli affects the dog, what his reactions are, and how severe his reactions are. It is also the appropriate time to formulate and implement beginning desensitization and habituation approaches that are specialized for him.

As you and the dog get to know one another, changes in habituation and desensitization approaches may have to be made. New fears may crop up and have to be dealt with. What you can and should expect is the unexpected. Develop flexibility in your programs and be surprised if there are no surprises. When a new problem arises, your calm, steady leadership will help the dog cope.

You will see gradual improvement in the dog's fear tolerance. Plateaus will be reached that may necessitate your reevaluation of approach. If a plateau is reached and the dog shows no interest in further learning, a pause in advancement can be replaced by play sessions or other exercise breaks. Repeat practice of successful behaviors already accomplished will maintain the dog's new knowledge.

It is okay to let the dog remain plateaued until he chooses to advance himself. Whenever he chooses to advance (through demonstrating curiosity, rather than fear, about novel situations), it is evident that the overall program is succeeding. If the breather time lags indefinitely, you will have to rethink the program and perhaps kick-start advancement with something new.

Above all, realize that all dogs can continue to improve and adjust over long periods of time. Some dogs may take years to overcome fears. But there is a difference between longer periods of gradual improvement and complete cessation of improvement.

WHAT TO SETTLE FOR

If the dog plateaus due to age, physical ailments, or cognitive limitations, you may have to settle for what she is willing or able to give and not expect more. For example, a fifteen-year-old dog may have some dementia that will never allow total eradication of her anxiety. At that point, the most comfortable, safe, and least challenging home will be the best fit for the dog.

Your sensitivity to each pet's limitations will help you determine appropriate acceptance of those limitations. It can be difficult to decide when to push for more and when to let hopes for advancement end. With experience, compassion, and awareness you can determine the most humane and realistic time to settle for what the dog can comfortably live with. Managing her life to the best scenario is the goal. Whatever you provide will probably be better than what she has experienced before, especially if she comes from a homeless or neglectful situation.

Spirit arrived at the sanctuary on a bright summer day, although it was no different in her eyes than any other day because she was blind. Spirit was lifted out of the rescue vehicle by two women and was placed in a large outside run. One of the women spoke kindly to her. The woman slowly led Spirit around on a leash so she could become familiar with the scents and boundaries of her area. Once her leash was removed, Spirit froze, afraid to move. In addition to the other woman, another dog that had been in the vehicle in the next cubicle was near; Spirit could hear and smell her. Spirit held her head at an angle, listening. The two people noticed this.

"Why is Spirit's head tilted like that?" asked a second woman.

"She's blind and has a neurological imbalance in her left ear canal," said the first.

"An elderly couple rescued and raised her. They were both placed in a nursing home, and no one wanted a dog with her issues."

Spirit felt two streams of hot breath, then the slight pressure of a fuzzy muzzle on her neck. She jumped. She could not see the other dog's body language and lived in constant anxiety when she smelled dogs nearby. She had been raised in isolation with her elderly people and had no intimate experience with her own kind.

"We put Spirit in with Snow. Snow is deaf. We thought they would be good partners. Snow's family could no longer afford to feed her."

Spirit heard the two women walk away. Snow was nearby but made no aggressive noises and her scent was calm when Spirit extended her tilted head for a sniff. The two dogs quickly learned to trust each other and became partners in their respective disabilities.

Spirit can now trot a funny lopsided gait and play with Snow. She follows the sounds of Snow's footfalls. Deaf Snow watches Spirit, knowing that if there is something to be frightened of, she can trust her blind friend to hear sounds of danger. Both dogs will remain together, loved by sanctuary staff and out of danger. Each dog has developed confidence in herself, affection for her dog friend, and trust in her caregivers. Despite their combined physical flaws, they live full and contented lives.

MOVING ON

Roadblocks such as cognitive, emotional, and physical ailments may make it necessary for you to accept the limitations of a dog and move on to areas of training that can be progressed in. All fearful dogs have psychological and/or physical limitations. Do what you can with the fears that are amenable to behavior modification and settle for managing the others. Help a fearful dog discover his strengths and concentrate on them so he can continue to learn. When it is apparent that he cannot do what you ask, find something he can do so he can find a way to obtain your praise.

Accepting limitations puts greater emphasis on the dog's need for your companionship in other ways. Although training time is bonding, once training is no longer possible, a peaceful environment and the physical availability of a trusted person will remain important to the dog.

Buddha, a twelve-year-old Tibetan Spaniel, was placed in his new owner's arms one month after he was abandoned at a large shelter by people he hardly knew. His elderly owner had passed away and the family did not know what to do with the old dog. No one wanted him. Buddha was processed through the shelter intake department. He was neutered, given inoculations, and had two molars pulled during a dental cleaning. Shortly afterwards, Buddha lost the use of his lower jaw and could not swallow water or keep food in his mouth. Shelter personnel did not notice, although he lost weight quickly.

No one thought Buddha had long to live, but his new owner wanted to provide him one last year of care and peace. She noticed how water dribbled out of his mouth when he tried to drink. She could only get food into him if she held it up and dropped it down his throat, as if she were feeding a baby bird. She quickly took him to a variety of veterinarians to find out why his jaw did not work.

Buddha was finally diagnosed with trigeminal neuropathy, a rare neurological disease caused by over-stimulation of the immune system resulting from multiple inoculations. Buddha's owner hand fed and watered him until his immune system quieted with medication and the nerves grew responsive again. When he could eat and drink properly, Buddha gained weight and became as active as a twelve-year-old dog with arthritis could.

It did not take long for Buddha's dementia to become obvious, but his new owner made adjustments to Buddha's life so he was not easily frightened by changes in his environment. He had ramps to go inside and outside his own dog door and there were three cats for company. Buddha eventually lost all of his hearing and most of his eyesight, yet his little heart kept motoring on, despite congestive heart failure and a heart murmur. He was not an affectionate dog, but he was accepted for the isolationist he was. He was fed well, received excellent medical care, was given soft chew toys, and had warm beds. Although he did not seem to appreciate it, companionship was available. Buddha's owner expected nothing else and respected the little grump and his needs. Her only wish was to give him a level of life quality for whatever time he had left.

Buddha passed away at home five years after he came to his new owner. Thanks to people who cared, his last five years were comfortable and peaceful.

HOW TO DETERMINE WHAT THE OPTIMAL LEVEL IS

When no progress in the training/desensitization/habituation program occurs, despite changes in the program, you must be willing to accept that the optimal level of development for that dog has been reached. Personal ego must not stand in the way of reality, and the dog should be left in peace. If his life is of high enough quality that he appears calmer and reasonably happy, take pride in the assistance you have been able to provide him. An optimal level of comfort for a fearful dog can happen when he is allowed to live without any further formal rehabilitation effort.

If placing the dog in a good home is the goal, screen potential adopters and look for those who will accept and tolerate the dog in his "as is" condition. Adopters who will take a fearful pet, regardless of his quirks, are nuggets of gold in the animal welfare world. Provide them with information regarding the work you have done with the dog and educate them in the behavior modification program the dog is familiar with to ensure a relatively smooth transition.

If the dog is yours, the bonding that has occurred during the work of developing your relationship should cement your acceptance of him. By the time you have reached your dog's optimal socialization level, you will know that the positive points of your relationship with him outweigh any troublesome idiosyncrasies.

Hercules was an emaciated nine-year-old Chihuahua stud dog when he was rescued during a raid on his Ohio puppy mill. The only time he had been touched by human hands was when he was snatched out of his wire cage and plopped into another cage with a female in heat. After mating, both were separated and returned to their respective prisons.

Transferred with fifty-five other dogs to a shelter, Hercules was subjected to the first veterinary care he had ever experienced. Due to advanced gum disease, all his teeth were pulled, which left his tongue lolling uncontrolled out one side of his mouth. He was neutered, given a barrage of inoculations, and medicated twice a day for an eye infection. After years of rarely being touched, suddenly, human hands were all over him, hurting him.

Hercules gained weight and his short hair gained sheen, but he remained shy and withdrawn. He was placed in a foster home for surgical recovery and socialization. There he was kept in a clean enclosure on a real floor. Hercules was frightened of the new flat, slippery surface, so his foster caretaker placed fluffy towels underfoot, which were not only good for traction, but also good for absorption.

Having lived his entire life in a wire mesh cage, Hercules had never learned to control his bowel or bladder.

The same day he arrived in his foster home, Hercules was joined by Mary Ann, an energetic, affectionate three-year-old Dachshund. Hercules immediately fell in love. Mary Ann loved people and it was obviously best for Hercules that she remain with him past her own surgical recovery to aid in his adjustment to life in a home.

After months of gentle socialization efforts by their foster caregiver, Hercules and Mary Ann were listed for adoption. Hercules still hated to be handled but he tolerated it and showed no fear aggression. He still hid under blankets in his enclosure but he followed Mary Ann into the yard through their own door. There he fearlessly investigated every corner of a world he had never seen. He galloped through grass, learned to lift his leg on rocks, and barked at squirrels, who were as small as he was. He and Mary Ann napped in the sunshine and lapped water from a fountain in the yard.

A young woman—prophetically named Hope—came to look at Mary Ann and Hercules. She was an experienced and loving adopter who understood the issues of longtime puppy mill dogs. She adopted Hercules and Mary Ann together, as had been stipulated by their caregiver and the shelter. They joined three other Chihuahuas, one Dachshund, and a Great Pyrenees dog in Hope's home. Hope accepted Hercules and knew his socialization advancement had reached its peak. Hercules lived with Hope, Mary Ann, and the other dogs for another year-and-a-half. He passed away from heart disease at home with his friends.

GIVING UP

When negative aspects of a dog's fearful condition outweigh the positive aspects of the relationship between him and his person, and when the quality of life for both is poor, the option of last resort may be to give up on the relationship.

When a fearful pet's quirks disrupt the owner's life to the point that the relationship deteriorates, which may cause the dog to behaviorally regress, finding another home may become necessary. If another person can be found who is better equipped to cope with the animal's behavior and willing to take him on, it may be better for all. A poor match between dog and owner is miserable for the dog and the person.

If you foster or train for a rescue organization professionally, it is your responsibility to find the right match for your student dog. When you work with a dog you plan to find an eventual home for, carefully research all aspects of compatibility between your dog and potential adopters. You know the dog better than anyone so be true to him. Poor matches between adopters and dogs are emotionally trying for both. Hold out for the best home you can find. Educate potential adopters to the dog's personality, energy level, behavior modification program, medical history, and personal needs.

If the adoption does not work out, be open to accepting the dog back and trying to place him again. If his first adopters give up on him, evaluate the reasons. Often, one unsatisfactory match does not dictate that the next will fail. Objectively evaluate the human component within the failure. Many dogs lose homes through no fault of their own. People can be notoriously fickle, a trait dogs do not and cannot have. If there is a true behavioral component on behalf of the dog, determine how to correct, manage, or accept it. Then help the next adopter enter the dog's life with open eyes and educate them thoroughly.

Follow up support for the adopters and the dog may be necessary to help him keep his new home. Your work does not stop on adoption day. Your responsibility to the dog you have brought so far is to help his new family continue his growth.

Digger loved to herd sheep. The Australian Shepherd spent his days running the fields that belonged to his beloved ranchman. He eagerly excavated rabbit holes and investigated prairie dog tunnels. He was an energetic digger and became expert at burying anything he found of value. He often galloped to the neighbor's ranch, and although he was shy around the people, he played with the three dogs that lived there. He always ran home when the ranch routine that was ingrained in his brain told him he was needed for chores.

When his owner was confined to a wheelchair, Digger brought the sheep in alone, with his master's whistle tweeting directions from the yard. After ranch hands closed the gates and the sheep work was done, Digger returned to lie at the ranchman's unmoving feet.

A big white vehicle with a flashing red light arrived one morning and took the ranchman away. Digger never saw him again. Soon after, Digger was left by a ranch hand at an animal shelter in the city. Confused and frightened, Digger paced the chain link barrier of his run—he had never known a fence that could confine him. His loneliness was exacerbated by his building, unused energy, and he panted and paced in restlessness and despair.

Digger was visited by a quiet woman. She took his leash and led him to her car. Intrigued, Digger jumped in. The lady let him out of her car into a small, neat front yard filled with flower beds. She let him explore her tidy little house and then they went into the fenced backyard, which was a little bigger than the front yard and also had beautiful flower gardens. Digger stayed with the lady.

The lady walked Digger twice a day around the block and through a park nearby. She was gone during the day, but Digger busied himself digging holes in the aromatic yard soil, trotting the fence line, and beating a path through the flowers. He also compulsively went in and out the dog door, leaving muddy clumps on the carpet inside, and his silky, long Aussie fur gathered in balls under the lady's furniture. When she had other people over, he hid under a shrub in the backyard. Through the weeks in the lady's home, Digger never had a single good, long, lung-expanding run, free of a leash and the weight of his lady at the end of it.

The lady became meaner. She yelled at him frequently when she returned home and during the evenings when she sat watching television while he tried to entice her to play with balls. When her temper flared, Digger scampered under the bed and cowered until she went to sleep. She bought a metal collar with prongs on it that stabbed his neck when he tried to greet other dogs in the park. Strange people made him uneasy and there were so many in the city. Although there were many dogs on leashes in the park, he had no dog friends to play with.

Digger's anxiety and unmet need for exercise culminated in a nervousness he could not control. He obsessively dug holes everywhere, which made the lady angrier. She spent less time with him outside, and he was not comfortable in the tiny house. He avoided her in every way he could.

Digger's lady returned him to the shelter. A new trainer worked with him and carefully sorted through adoption applications. Then she made a call to a man and spoke with him for a long time.

That new man visited Digger the next afternoon. The many scents on the man's shoes and pant legs brought familiar memories to Digger. He whined and rubbed against the legs that smelled like his former home. When the man leashed Digger, he compliantly jumped into the man's vehicle. The man jabbered in kind tones until he stopped the vehicle.

Digger looked out. He found himself on another ranch far outside of town. Wide fields beckoned him for a run. In those fields there were sheep! Digger's instinct and training burst through and he jumped out of the truck. He ran and circled the sheep herd. As he brought them in, Digger looked at his new man as though to ask, "Where do you want these?"

Surprised and pleased, the man opened a gate to an enclosure and praised Digger as the sheep streamed in. Digger remained with the man and had work, companionship, and other dogs to mentor and play with. The unique match between Digger and the man was successful and neither gave up on the other.

―⁄ᶥ∖―

Conclusion

When a fearful dog and a compassionate person come together in a dovetailing of trust, affection, and a comfortable bubble of familiarity, a relationship of rare, enduring, and endearing quality is established. Most behaviorists who favor fearful pets continue in their missions to save lives. Owners seek out shy pets to be their next family member. Trainers return to the shelter, sanctuary, or rescue for another timid student.

Despite patches of frustration, sorrow, confusion, anger, hope, and happiness, the person who accepts a fearful dog into their life will find fulfillment unlike any other. When you have saved the life of a confused and innocent creature and shown that animal what a quality life can be, there will be quality meaning in your own life. You have made a difference.

The human psyche requires us to be of use and to be needed. It inspires us to protect, love, and advocate for the less fortunate. We find this fulfillment and purpose in our marriages, partnerships, children, families, communities, churches, and places of employment. We volunteer, work overtime, seek public service, and enter altruistic activities to give of ourselves. As St. Francis of Assisi—the patron saint of animals—put it, "For only in giving can we receive."

Unfortunately, there are many more dogs who need you, whether you are a professional rehabilitator, foster caregiver, or an adopter. For most professionals, there are no degrees, no certificates, and no titles to place at the end of your name on a business card. Yet, you should take time to reflect on what you have accomplished each time a dog finds a lifelong loving home after your work with her.

When you open your heart and home to foster a fearful dog, know that you are saving that dog's life. Most fearful dogs languish in commercial facilities. Their sensitive natures cannot tolerate the overstimulation of impersonal and often overcrowded kennels. Timid dogs need personal attention, quiet, routine, and a familiar person to interact with. They cannot thrive without the intimate trust that a home environment can provide. You, therefore, are a crucial key to the happy endings these types of dogs can find, if given time.

For those who adopt and give homes to dogs rejected by others for their quirks, there are no medals or kudos. If you have adopted a fearful dog and have committed your heart and life to her, you should be proud of the fact that you are among the caring cadre of adopters who take on this challenging and rewarding role.

All of us are important cogs in the wheel that moves the jagged climb of human evolution upwards. You are an integral part of a quiet, peaceful army of kind, compassionate, and loving people who were called to this special and imperative work.

When your adventure with one fearful dog is completed, take a deep breath, and gather up your motivation, love, optimism, tools, and books—hopefully including this one. Then go find another fearful dog who needs you and what you do.

-⁄|⟨-

Glossary of Terms

(as used in the context of this book)

Advocate — to plead a case for another; support;
vindicate; plead in favor of

Antecedent — the presentation of a request for a behavior

Anthropomorphism — assignment of human emotional and
cognitive interpretations to animals

Baseline — beginning; base; a place to start from

Behavior — action; way of conducting oneself in response to
a stimulus

Canine — pertaining to dog-like species

Catatonic — emotional, physical, cognitive ceasing of
reaction or awareness; emotional shutdown

Chains of Command — multiple activities resulting from
minimal requests

Command — request for action or behavior

Confused — unable to comply due to ignorance of request;
perplexed

Consequence — natural or necessary result

Cue — physical or verbal signal

Curiosity — to seek new knowledge

Decompress — to release from pressure

Desensitize — to make less sensitive or reactive

Displacement — indirect activity used to distract

Enrichment — any technique designed to improve the functioning of a dog through environmental modifications

Extinction Burst — attempts to obtain attention by frequent and intense performance of an undesirable behavior

Fear Memory — associating an event or thing with a fearful reaction that is always remembered

Feral — wild; untamed; undomesticated

Flood — to overwhelm with stimuli to the point of panic

Fluency — automatic comprehension and connected action; done without undue thinking

Freeze — to halt all movement

Genetics — inherited traits

Generalize — to transfer knowledge from one scenario to another

Habituation — to become familiar with

Hardwired — natural instinct; brain function by genetics; inborn

Indirect Desensitization — frequent natural activity that results in lower reactivity

Instinctual Fascination — mesmerized attention that is not controlled by logic

Jackpot — considerable quantity; more than usual

Loaded — to train to a certain result; to associate a thing or place with a particular outcome

Mirror — imitate

Motivator — impetus to create an action

Naturally Occurring Behavior — breed, species, and sex behavior that is considered typical; natural physical action such as walking, running, playing, sitting, laying down, relaxing, sleeping, etc.

Neotinized — to keep in perpetual child-like or immature state

Noise Markers — specific sounds used in training for purposes of correction or reward

Overload — to overwhelm with stimuli that causes stress reaction

Pack — group; family

Pack Juggling — canine social flexibility or change in hierarchy

Pheromones — secreted or excreted chemicals that trigger social responses in members of the same species; capable of acting outside the body of the secreting individual to impact the behavior of the receiving individual

Predator — an animal that pursues, chases, kills, and eats another animal

Pre-training — preparing for formal structure of training utilizing and rewarding already occurring behaviors

Prey — any animal seized to be devoured

Prey Drive — desire and action to catch prey

Primary Motivators — tools (such as food treats) used in the beginning stages of training to help teach the dog the connection between the request for a behavior and the performance of that behavior

Randomize — to vary without pattern

Reboot — to clear the slate; shut down then restart

Recall — to come from another location to the source that calls

Recovery — to cease negative reaction; to go back to normal

Redirection — to change direction; start from one and go to another

Reinforcement — consequence that encourages repeat performance

Reinforcer — something that strengthens and/or encourages continuation

Reliability — consistency; trustworthiness; dependable for performance

Secondary Motivator — a replacement for a primary motivator; often randomized to provide higher motivation for positive behavioral performance; most often verbal praise or physical affection

Setup — to manufacture

Set up, to — situation that would not happen at that time or in that way independently

Stalk — to follow with malevolent intention

Startle — sudden, sharp fear

Socialize — ability to abide by community standards; to accept the environmental limitations and rules of the society one lives within

Socialization — the process by which one is taught to fit into society

Stimuli — multiple objects or situations that stimulate reaction

Stimulus — single object or situation that stimulates reaction

Trading — exchanging one item for another

White Factor — three or more different genetic combinations resulting in three alleles of the same recessive gene; often accompanied by deafness and/or blindness

White Noise — a flat spectrum sound used to decrease tension

About the Author

Sunny Weber has over 25 years of experience in animal welfare advocacy. She has experience in rescue, fostering, medical care, service and therapy dog evaluation and training, shelter and sanctuary work and specializes in the rehabilitation of fearful animals. Sunny has rehabilitated then re-homed hundreds of dogs, cats and horses.

A professional humane educator, Sunny consults with animal welfare professionals as well as adopters and has developed educational programs that address all ages regarding the need for compassion and care of domestic and wild animals. She writes extensively on animal issues in news, fiction, non-fiction, investigative reporting, public relations, fundraising, and blogs.

Sunny has owned several businesses and has backgrounds in speaking, marketing, sales, teaching, management, personal service, and public relations.

Sunny lives with dogs, cats and parakeets. Their yard is a Certified Backyard Habitat for birds, squirrels, rabbits, pollinators, and any other creature with fur or feathers who wanders in.